When Students Protest

When Students Protest

Universities in the Global South

Edited by
Judith Bessant, Analicia Mejia Mesinas,
and Sarah Pickard

ROWMAN & LITTLEFIELD
Lanham • Boulder • New York • London

Credits and acknowledgments for material borrowed from other sources, and reproduced with permission, appear on the appropriate page within the text.

Published by Rowman & Littlefield
An imprint of The Rowman & Littlefield Publishing Group, Inc.
4501 Forbes Boulevard, Suite 200, Lanham, Maryland 20706
www.rowman.com

British Library Cataloguing in Publication Information Available

Library of Congress Cataloging-in-Publication Data

Names: Bessant, Judith, editor. | Mejia Mesinas, Analicia, 1988- editor. | Pickard, Sarah, editor.
Title: When students protest / edited by Judith Bessant, Analicia Mejia Mesinas and Sarah Pickard.
Description: Lanham, Maryland : Rowman & Littlefield Publishers, 2021. | Includes bibliographical references and index. | Contents: [v. 1]. Secondary and high schools—[v. 2]. Universities in the global North—[v. 3]. Universities in the global South. | Summary: "Student political action has been a major and recurring feature of politics across the globe throughout the past century. Students have been involved in a full range of public issues, from anti-colonial movements, anti-war campaigns, civil rights and pro-democracy movements to campaigns against neoliberal policies, austerity, racism, misogyny and calls for climate change action. Yet student protest actions are frequently dismissed by political elites and others as 'adolescent mischief' or manipulation of young people by duplicitous adults. This occurs even as many working in government, traditional media and educational organisations attempt to suppress student movements. Much of mainstream scholarly work has also deemed student politics as undeserving of intellectual attention. These three edited volumes of books help set the record straight."—Provided by publisher.
Identifiers: LCCN 2021014407 (print) | LCCN 2021014408 (ebook) | ISBN 9781786611765 (v. 1 ; cloth) | ISBN 9781786611772 (v. 1 ; paperback) | ISBN 9781786611796 (v. 2 ; cloth) | ISBN 9781786611802 (v. 2 ; paperback) | ISBN 9781786611826 (v. 3 ; cloth) | ISBN 9798881801021 (v. 3 ; paperback) | ISBN 9781786611789 (v. 1 ; epub) | ISBN 9781786611819 (v. 2 ; epub) | ISBN 9781786611840 (v. 3 ; epub)
Subjects: LCSH: Student movements. | Protest movements. | High school students—Political activity. | College students—Political activity.
Classification: LCC LA186 .W44 2021 (print) | LCC LA186 (ebook) | DDC 378.1/981—dc23
LC record available at https://lccn.loc.gov/2021014407
LC ebook record available at https://lccn.loc.gov/2021014408

Contents

Acknowledgments

The idea of this book was conceived back in 2017–2018 when the three editors, long interested in student activism, detected a new kind of energy and focus on student action for climate change campaigns across the globe. Since 2018, the scale, intensity, and frequency of student political action has increased substantially. Even in 2020, a year marked by the COVID-19 pandemic, this seems to have merely generated a raft of new and creative forms of political expression and practice on the part of students.

We would like to thank a number of people without whom these three books would not have happened. First, all the authors in the three volumes, many of whom are, or were, participants in the action they wrote about. We thank you for your commitment to the project, your insights, talent, effort and especially we are grateful for your patience with our often-repeated requests for revisions to chapters sometimes in difficult circumstances. It has been a great pleasure collaborating with you and we wish you well.

Each of us also thank our good colleagues and students for the support you have provided during this project. We acknowledge the support of the universities that employed us as academics while we undertook this project. For Judith, it is Royal Melbourne Institute of Technology (RMIT) University, Melbourne, Australia. For Analicia, it is the Department of Criminal Justice and the School of Behavioral and Applied Sciences at Azusa Pacific University, United States of America. For Sarah, it is the Université Sorbonne Nouvelle—Paris 3, France.

Special thanks also go to Rob Watts who provided enormous support through this project and especially during the "Dubai incident," when Judith was out of action for a little while as the first batch of chapters came tumbling in. We are truly appreciative.

We would also like to thank our friends and families.

To the students across the world from primary school through to universities, who were interviewed and whose actions and ideas provide much of the material in these three volumes, we also express our thanks.

Last and importantly, we thank Rowman & Littlefield for having faith in this project and seeing the promise in the initial proposal we sent some years ago. In particular, we thank Dhara Snowden and Rebecca Anastasi for their ongoing professional and always helpful support.

Chapter 1

Student Protest in the Global South

Introductory Essay

Judith Bessant, Analicia Mejia Mesinas,
and Sarah Pickard

Editors, like writers, necessarily deal with words. As Hannah Arendt noted, the words we employ do matter because politics is about how we use words and how we act (1958). Whether as editors or writers, we hope that by using words thoughtfully, we can grasp what is actually happening around us, some of the facts and features of our world. This allows us to talk about the world with some clarity. These thoughts came to mind early on, as we three editors began thinking how to design the three volumes dealing with student protest.[1]

From the beginning of this edited book project, we had two questions in mind. First, when students protest, what do they think about and do? Second, when students protest, how do other players like governments, educational authorities, the police and security forces, the media, and communities respond? We also appreciated the value of distinguishing between different kinds of student protest actions, their repertoires of contention (Tilly 1986, 1995), the diversity of issues that concerned them and the resources they drew on.

We also noticed how primary and secondary education students are so often overlooked or just lumped together with further and higher or tertiary education students, while giving little consideration of their differences. With this in mind, we created a specific volume (Volume 1) focusing on primary and secondary school students' protest and two others (Volumes 2 and 3) about when students in tertiary institutions or universities protest.

The key themes we used to order the volumes and chapters seemed to emerge naturally with relatively clearly demarcated boundaries. What counted as protest action, what constituted a primary, secondary, and tertiary student seemed relatively straightforward, while acknowledging a few differences across national and regional borders.

Of course, we also thought, given the spread of student action that we needed to take a global view. Added to this was the observation that the literature on protest actions also primarily focused on activity in the "Global North." It soon became apparent as authors from around the world responded to our invitation to contribute to the book, that we had attracted the interest of a significant number of authors from the "Global South." We became excited about the opportunity to shed light on the action of students and scholars in these places, and believed a volume dedicated to politics in the "Global South" was essential. However, our decision to use the language of the "Global South" acknowledged that this is a contentious and contested category.

LANGUAGE COMPLEXITY

As many philosophers have long appreciated and as many social scientists understand, there is no magical way to make our words and the world align either simply or easily. This is partly due to the ways language works. When we speak, write, read or listen, we use words as names of things, or to describe a state of affairs, or to see similarities or differences. We do this using metaphors, or performatively (as calls to action), or evaluatively and politically.

Our use of language is always tricky in part because many of the words we use have numerous meanings. Added to this complexity is the world itself or "reality." It is a world that seems to be made up of tangible hard objects, but when we look closer, it becomes apparent that this is not the case. To compound these complexities, the world and our language are constantly entangled in each other. Our words *are in* the world, with each changing in the course of constant mutual interaction. In short, words have effects on the world, which in turn influence our language.

It helps editors and writers to appreciate these points about language. In our case, given the way we decided to use the categories "Global South" and "Global North" to design the three volumes, we faced the task of considering what these categories meant and where these categories came from.

When people talk about the "Global North" and the "Global South," do they use political-economic, geo-political, or geographic criteria? Or is the "global south" a cartographic or map-based metaphor? If so, does this imply that the term "global south" is neither literal nor descriptive. Or is it more like how we used older metaphors, such as "the third world," or "developing countries," or now "emerging countries' economies"? Do the categories of Global South and Global North refer to other "sociohistorical factors" like socioeconomic or political "development" or "Western democracies"? Or does it make more sense to understand the "Global South" and the "Global North" historically, in terms of the long-term effects of colonialism? Is it a way of talking about an imperial history? One way of getting some clarity is to trace the linage of these concepts.

For centuries after 1492, the year when Christopher Columbus (*Cristoforo Colombo)* was supposed to have "discovered" the Americas, various words and metaphors were used by Europeans and later North Americans, such as empire, colonies, natives, slavery, and the planting of "civilization," which included the imposition of colonial languages and the suppression of indigenous languages.

They were metaphors that functioned within stories about the dramatic and assumed benevolent spread of European military, education, legal systems, religion (courtesy of missionaries), economic control of lands and people across the globe, referred to as "civilization." All these were put together into an eighteenth-century colonial story about world history as progress to justify the actions of the occupying powers, while at the same time supressing local ingenious worldviews and narratives.

There are various difficulties about writing from a southern perspective that parallel the difficulties of assuming that the northern perspective is the only (i.e., universal) perspective. After all, there is no "nowhere place" from which to write. As Todorov (1999) observed, the European conquest of the Americas was partly a reflection of the absence in meso-America of any written culture. The subsequent evolution of southern theory has always been characterized by a reliance on northern categories and assumptions.

However, by the late nineteenth and early twentieth centuries, and after slavery was legally abolished, first in the British Empire in 1834 (Slavery Abolition Act 1933) and then in America in 1865 (Thirteenth Amendment to the US Constitution), the vocabulary began changing. The change in language was a development that reflected how nationalist, anti-colonial, and later Marxist revolutionary movements gathered momentum internationally. The Bolshevik leader Lenin used the language of imperialism in 1917 to refer to the effects of global capitalism. He did this using categories such as colonialism, racism, hegemony and exploitation to invoke what he saw as the solution—namely revolution. Elsewhere, nationalist leaders of independence movements, like Gandhi, Rivera, Atatürk, Sun Yat-sen, and Connolly, in countries such as India, Cuba, Turkey, and Ireland, redefined liberal-democratic and socialist notions of national sovereignty and self-determination to initiate and mobilize movements intended to evict the European colonial powers.

From the end of the Second World War (1945) to the mid-1950s, various anti-colonial and Marxist movements in Africa and Asia either eradicated the obvious aspects of colonialism, or were on a path to achieving it. The onset of the Cold War, a global conflict between liberal capitalism and communism, encouraged Western leaders, policy-makers and experts to adopt a vocabulary used to mark the difference between countries and regions according to levels of economic development.

During the Cold War (1948–1989), a typical way of carving up the globe was by the terms "First World," or industrialized and capitalist (such as Australia, Japan, New Zealand, United States of America, Western Europe), the "Second World," made up of industrialized communist countries (the Soviet Union, Bulgaria, Hungary, Poland, etc.) and the "Third World," or everywhere else (Africa, Asia, the Caribbean, Central America, South America, Middle East, etc.).

Foreign policy discussion increasingly came to be described in terms of "development." The idea of underdeveloped was coined officially in the 1951 United Nations (UN) document *Measures for the Economic Development of Under-Developed Countries* (UN 1951).

Among the assumptions informing this language and thinking was the idea that the newly liberated former colonies could be protected from the ravages of communism, if they followed the Western path of "progress" toward economic "modernization" and wealth generation.

Here we see powerful metaphors operating. Words like "developed," "less developed," "developing," and "least developed" regions, drew on the basic metaphors of "development" and "underdevelopment." These words imply that a pathway (or course) of development exists and unfolds in stages designed to arrive at an optimal endpoint. From 1945, new institutions like the International Monetary Fund (IMF) and the World Bank became central to the Bretton Woods monetary system—all designed to provide capital for this project and to expand international trade courtesy of a payments system. Yet, as the sociologist Immanuel Wallerstein argued, there were significant inequalities between "core" nations, "semi-periphery" nations and "periphery" nations of this new or "modern world system" (1974–78), which seemed to describe what was happening, while also highlighting the dynamic connectedness within the global system.

The collapse or death of the Soviet empire in the late 1980s meant the end of the Cold War. Western liberal-democratic states and institutions, such as the World Bank and the IMF, appeared to have defeated "communism" and celebrated their triumph. The world, so it seemed, was witnessing the victory of liberal capitalism and the "end of history" described in terms of the Cold War conflict between old rival ideologies (namely communist USSR and capitalist United States) (Fukuyama 1992).

For the next two decades, many academics and others used the vocabulary of globalization to communicate the idea that all nations were now part of an interconnected web of relationships and on a common path to progress (Wallerstein 2000; Steger 2017). Many leaders and experts promoted their dreams about the value and benevolent spread of finance capital and its new, debt-based assets (e.g., derivatives), and the new digital technologies, like the Internet, which were shrinking the globe. The "Washington consensus" was a watershed moment that saw the advent of neoliberal imaginary take hold slowly but surely across many parts of the globe. It was a worldview that privileged the "free market" and brought forth rising unemployment, reduced wages and pensions and the regular use of austerity policies. It was a worldview that won support across much of the political spectrum which included labor parties (e.g., Australia, New Zealand, United Kingdom), conservative parties (e.g., Germany, the United Kingdom, and the United States of America) to socialist (France and Sweden) and postcolonial regimes (Brazil, Chile, India, South Africa). At the same time, many of the "developed" Western economies began deindustrializing and coming to accept the "knowledge economy." Meanwhile, places like Brazil, Russia, India, China, and South Africa (BRICS) became the manufacturing powerhouses in the new global economy.

Concomitantly, the distinction was made increasingly between richer, more developed, industrialized countries in the Northern Hemisphere and poorer, less developed countries in the Southern Hemisphere. The terms "North" and "South" were used by the Independent Commission on International Development Issues in their report titled: *North-South: A Programme for Survival*. (Brandt 1980).[2]

It was at this point terms like the "global south" and "global north" were generally used.

The "Global South" and the "Global North"

International agencies like the World Bank often refer to "typical" "global south" countries in Africa, Asia, Oceania, Latin America, and the Caribbean.[3] Yet, if we use identifying features of the "Global South" like low average levels of income and education, significant poverty and unemployment rates, heightened rates of crime and illicit drug use, or reduced life expectancy, we can see that the boundaries that demarcate "Global North" and "Global South" are no longer clearly or sharply delineated.

Clearly, problems like poverty, crime, unemployment, among others, are also found in many "developed" or "Global North" nations. That is, using criteria that indicate a prevalence of poverty or high crime rates to determine whether a country is part of the Global South or North is problematic because some countries "in the north" in Europe like Greece, and regions like some parts of the south of Italy. We might also point to subsistence living standards of some indigenous communities in remote northern Australia where levels of poverty, preventable disease, mortality, and suicide rates are unacceptably high. Then there is the United States, the richest nation in the world, where many Americans do not enjoy the same living standards of people in other developed nations (Piketty 2020). Alternately, if we use Europe as the reference point for the "Global North," what of nations in the Southern Hemisphere such as Australia, Chile, and New Zealand, which have large middle-classes and sophisticated economies, but geographically are in the Southern Hemisphere?

Given all this, it can be that the "Global North" and "Global South" categories are not straightforward objective descriptors of discrete, well-bounded objective nation-states or areas. Rather, they are categories that are deeply political and metaphoric representations. Like all metaphors, they function to structure our thinking and encourage us to see the world in particular ways. The global south-north metaphors invite us, for example, to see the world in which the European nations occupy ostensibly the prime real estate in the north, enjoying the positional advantage of living on "top of the world," while the southern realm is underneath, or "down under"—with resonances of the underworld as a space of pain, deprivation, and devoid of hope, but also inferiority. The metaphor of the "Global North" can also highlight the supposed accomplishment of successful "economic development" producing "wealthy" societies that adopted financial and service economies, enjoying the "benefits" of open markets sustained by neoliberal policy regimes, modern digital technologies and public services. But the "Global South" designates relatively poor, largely agrarian or pre-industrialized nations yet to achieve successful modernization or development. As metaphors, they can also be used to refer to patterns of political stability in the Global North and instability in the Global South.

These metaphors also offer inaccurate accounts of what is happening. Global diversity is such that it cannot be subsumed under two, or even a few key concepts. The countries of the world are too diverse to separate easily into two classifications: the "Global South," and the "Global North," signifying "developed" or "non-developed." This does not, however, mean we should stop using these metaphors completely? There is no easy answer to this question. One way of getting some clarity on such questions is to draw on social theory or specifically "Southern Theory."

Southern Theory

Writers like Gramsci (2006), Spivak (1988), and Said (1993) contributed to developing "southern theory." Connell's work provides the most comprehensive account and has been used as a basis for other research (Connell 2007, see also Meekosha 2008, 2011; Gale 2009; Jazeel and McFarlane 2010; Keim 2011; Alcadipani et al. 2012; Vaughan 2013).

Connell asks a helpful question: How does social thought and human action happen in particular places (2007, vii)? It is, as she says, a question often overlooked, due to the tendency to assume there is and can only be one, universal body of knowledge, concepts, and methods: those created in the "Global North." According to Connell, "southern theory" can help those working in the social sciences to better serve democratic purposes globally. She argues that historically, the mainstream conventional social sciences proposed versions of "northern theory" produced by people working in Anglo-American or northern or metropolitan centers. This observation highlights the value of seeing the North and South metaphorical distinction in terms of *relations between the periphery and the centre (metropole) that shape knowledge and knowledge-making practices*. It is a perspective that is directly relevant to this volume.

For Connell, "north-south" or "metropolitan-periphery" distinctions are not tight or sharply bounded categories that refer objectively or descriptively to empirical states of affairs. Rather, they "emphasize relations [of] authority, exclusion, inclusion, hegemony, partnership, sponsorship, appropriation between intellectuals and institutions in the metropole and those in the world periphery" (Connell 2007, x–ix). In other words, historically, the dominant forms of knowledge, the governing concepts used to describe events and different kinds of people are northern in origin with the assumption they are universally applicable and superior.

With this in mind, it is critical when talking about global student action to acknowledge the dominance of northern knowledge making and the conceptual frames used to describe and understand key concepts like "politics," "education," or "citizenship," and different kinds of young people, such as the "child," the "adolescent," "young adult," "schoolchild," pupil, student and "youth" more widely (Sukarieh and Tannock 2018; Pickard 2019; Bessant 2021; Swartz et al. 2021).

Connell's southern theory can be used to challenge three consequences of northern theory and knowledge. They are (i) the claim of universality; (ii) reading from the center; (iii) grand erasures.

In what follows, we identify and briefly elaborate on these three concepts/consequences, while considering their implications for understanding student protest action, young people and responses to their action by the state and others.

The first is the claim of universality.

(i) Universality

"Real" (northern) knowledge and theory is predominantly assumed to be universal or globally relevant and true, while all else is peripheral or irrelevant and untrue. Embedded within the social sciences like economics, sociology, or political science are specific horizons or perspectives that help to constitute "social problems" that are actually based on northern ways of seeing and knowing the world, "while pretending to be universal knowledge" (Connell 2007, vii; Heidegger 1962). The assumption is that "all societies are knowable in the same way and from the same point of view," which is typically white, middle class, and male (Connell 2007, 44). In short, northern knowledge is epistemically, methodologically, and thus "scientifically" superior.

As mentioned above, core concepts directly relevant to this edited collection, such as the student, child, and youth all have northern origins and shape how we come to know and understand the actions of student activists. They are concepts or knowledge represented as universal and are then operationalized to inform local political institutional and socio-legal practices (e.g., enduring commitment to specific universal education principles, application of universal design curricula, welfare and medical interventions, the increasing application of "user pays" education). This is done in ways that displace local knowledge and practice that can be inappropriate for understanding the global south (Chakrabarty 2012). They are categories constructed within specific milieus and transferred to various sites for the purpose of governing and constituting certain kinds of "individuals," which in turn work to serve various state and other socioeconomic and political interests (Cooper et al. 2018; Swartz et al. 2021).

The effect of this universality can be seen in the prevailing euro-centrism of the natural and social sciences that also pervades much of our common-sense thinking. It is also evident if we observe how the "founding fathers" theories, social analysis, and worldviews of modern disciplines (like philosophy, sociology, economics, politics, psychology) are built on a universalized and naturalized Western "model" of the world. These perspectives typically work to sustain inequalities and fantasies along with global influences on local communities (Bühler-Niederberger and van Krieken 2008). Critics point to disciplines like history, sociology, and developmental psychology, in which it is claimed that societies and people or "individuals" with very different pasts and cultures can be comprehended in terms of universal "stages of development," transition, or "developmentalism" (e.g., Sukarieh and Tannock 2018, 451–469).

(ii) Reading from the Centre

"Reading from the centre" refers to the practice of interpreting the world from the northern perspective, which is regarded as the norm by those that employ it. Hence, the typical and silent assumption is that we can understand history as a "succession" of events in time, told in terms "of periods like pre-modern to modern or pre-capitalist to capitalist." It is a story that assumes that what is actually a metropolitan experience is universal (Connell 2007, 45). Such readings aspire to universality, overriding the specificities of the context, time, or space. In this way, they exclude, make invisible or attempt to normalize all those who do not fit the universal educational developmental norm or average.

This also means that researchers and theorists from the south or the periphery are excluded, rarely cited, and often their ideas not considered a legitimate part of theoretical dialogue in the Global North. This can be seen in the southern scholars whose insights are rarely used to inform in the literature of politics and student politics and indeed young people. As Cooper, Swartz, and Mahali (2019) point out, "90% of the world's youth live in Africa, Latin America or developing countries in Asia, while the overwhelming majority of research occurs at institutions in the global North." Moreover, the "differences between the lives of those living in the global north and the global south are so profound that many of the theories we use to understand the lives of young people are meaningless in non-Western contexts" (Nilan 2011 cited in Furlong 2013, 228).

The practice of reading from the centre can also be seen in the ways those who work in the social and natural sciences overlook the distinctive features of their grounds for knowing. This is evident in the failure to recognize how in their own practice they "read from the centre," make sweeping gestures that work to exclude and make grand erasures (Connell 2007).

(iii) Grand Erasures

The idea of grand erasures refers to the way the relationship between theoretical frames and "empirical" knowledge are obliterated. When empirical knowledge derives entirely or mainly from the "metropole" (the centre) and addresses problems experienced in the north (metropole), the effect is the erasure of the experiences and voices of people who are not from the north or not within the metropole (Connell 2007, 46).

One subtle but nonetheless powerful effect of erasures resulting from the claim of having universal knowledge (which is in fact based on the experiences of a privileged minority claiming to speak for everyone) is that it silences and renders invisible many people and communities. This occurs globally (in north and south relations) and locally, for example, in relations between local elites and socially disadvantaged and marginalized groups such as young people (Charlesworth 2000).

In this way, we read and hear much about student action of the 1960s in Europe (France, Germany, United Kingdom), but rarely in the Global North do we read of the student action in Argentina or Bangladesh. How might our understandings of student protest actions deepen if we were to more thoughtfully engage within scholarship in these areas?

It was this idea that suggested the value of reaching out to authors who were also participants in the actions they documented, and encouraged writers from countries recognized as coming from the "Global South" such as Argentina, Brazil, Chile, and India. It is an approach that is quite distinct from having the actions of student documented exclusively by outside observers—and authors from the north—which historically has been the dominant practice in the social sciences. We did this to encourage knowledge making that is informed by insider experiences of events, by how they identified themselves and others and saw the world.

Politically and ethically, this matters especially if those insider accounts are provided by students themselves. We say this because we see value in listening to students talk about their experiences of education and politics, as well as to have them document those experiences and encounters. Their contributions helped to build our analysis and understandings of student actions across the globe. It is part of an ethical-political project committed to promoting those who normally find themselves as the "object" of research that generates knowledge about them, but about which they have over if any input.

This approach also matters because it provides accounts of the specific political issues or social problems in question, whether they be university management practices, fee hikes or broader socioeconomic or environmental issues. Such perspectives enrich dialogue while respecting in a very practical way the principle of subsidiary. An approach that encourages a plurality of divergent and contesting views and knowledge-making practices has benefits for those interested in democratic ideals, and cooperative action.

There are also practical benefits for policy-makers, politicians, and others interested in a clearer understanding of the issues at hand from the position of those experiencing them. Among other things, this helps in gleaning a clearer framing or understanding of the problem, which in turn helps ensure responses are effective and built on experiences and views of those experiencing them.[4] Importantly, insider accounts from the Global South produce different kinds of knowledge and offer quite different accounts to the knowledge created by outsider's imaginings of what took place and why.

In these three volumes, we highlight the value of reinstating the distinctive voices and experiences of people such as students, and specifically, in this Volume II, we highlight the value of focusing on student activism across the "Global South." Indeed, this observation about grand erasures points to the value of not treating the distinction between the north and south as a literal geographic representation of the world.

We are pleased then that many of the authors who were also political actors provide insider accounts of their actions. They provide valuable firsthand insight into what happens when students protest. These kinds of accounts are not found to the degree that they ought to be in the social science disciplines such as politics, sociology, economics, and policy studies coming out of the global north.

CHAPTER SUMMARIES: STUDENT PROTEST ACTIONS IN THE GLOBAL SOUTH

The chapters in this volume focus primarily on Brazil, Chile, India, Mexico, Nigeria, and Sri Lanka and mostly cover the decade from 2009 to 2019.

Chapter 2, "Breaking Routines toward Conservatism? The 2013 Protests in Brazil," is authored by Enzo Bello, Gustavo Capela, and Rene José Keller. In this chapter, the authors explore the relationship between the historic and months long protests of 2013, led by young people and students, where millions of people took to the streets, and the rise of conservatism in Brazil. The chapter questions, how the country went from these widespread protests to the election of a far right and conservative president? To answer this often-contested question, the authors also consider what led to the student protests, what happened during the protests, and what were the key consequences from those actions. It is a chapter that draws on auto-ethnographic, supplemented by a critical review of the literature, and mainstream and social media during the time of the protests.

Chapter 3, "The Student Movement in Chile: Normalizing Protest and Opening Up Political Space," by Sofia Donoso and Nicolás Somma considers the rise of social movements and protest in Chile since the 2000s, following a significant period of considerable political disenchantment, especially from young people, after democracy was reinstated in 1990. In this context and after years of being demobilized, many students began raising questions about the education system and political institutions leading to a series of mass demonstrations. In 2011, high school and university students engaged in a series of actions calling for quality public and free education. Student leaders also argued for broader political reforms to Chile's democracy. The chapter documents how students along with other social movements contributed to the reshaping of various policies fields and political practices.

Chapter 4 by Pablo Santibáñez-Rodríguez documents the 2015–2016 occupations led by secondary students that contested the Educational National Assessment System in Chile. The chapter titled "Defending Education: Student Resistance to the Educational National Assessment System in Chile" identifies the varied ways students challenged the country's education policy, specifically the way the assessment had become part of a broader neoliberal move to marketize education. The chapter analyzes the traditional and digital protests of students, studying what they said, what they did, and how they represented themselves as "champions of the public system." In providing some context, Santibáñez-Rodríguez also documents the government's neoliberal educational policy that catalyzed the school occupations. Significantly, it was an agenda used by the state to mobilize public opinion against the students, and to usher in the "Secure Classroom" legislation. It was a move that increased tensions between students wanting quality education and proponents of the neoliberal educational imaginary.

Chapter 5, "Student Political Action and Activism in Contemporary Nigeria," by Joseph Egwurube examines how students in Nigeria organize themselves within universities and nationally paying close attention to the claims they make. Egwurube notes that although university students make up a relatively small of the overall Nigerian population, they are an undoubtable active minority, with a significant history of expressing their concerns about decisions made by the university manager and other government authorities. In documenting the various roles students play as they contest national regimes and their leaders, Egwurube observes how students' interests are not confined to higher education, but extend to general economic, social, and political issues.

Chapter 6, "(No) Right to Protest? Student Activism at Public Universities in India in the Modi Era," is authored by Nisha Thapliyal. Thapliyal writes how, since the 2014 election victory of Narendra Modi and his Hindu nationalist political party, public university campuses across India have been in a constant state of political ferment. She documents how both reactionary and progressive student groups have exercised their right to protest with a vengeance during this time. Student action is centered around the marketization and commodification of public higher education, and violence against women and Dalits (caste-based discrimination). Drawing on various sources including interviews, published activist narratives, news media reports, legal judgments, and academic commentary, Thapliyal maps the diverse modes of student political protests. Attention is then given to responses to that action and specifically the efforts by authorities such as university administrations, police, judiciary, and corporate news media to discipline and contain that dissent.

Chapter 7, " 'They've Completely Criminalized Us': Interrogating Student Activism in the Tamil Diaspora," is written by Meena Kandiah. This chapter is about the Sri Lankan civil war and the subsequent promises by the Sri Lankan government to provide justice and accountability for abuses during that war. It was a war that saw Sri Lankan armed forces drive the Liberation Tigers of Tamil Eelam, a proscribed separatist military organization, and

Tamil civilians within the separatist-controlled areas, into a tiny pocket of land. It was a time marked by mass atrocities, injuries, and the large-scale displacement of people. As the civil war peaked, we saw a mass mobilization of younger Tamil students, comprised of those who were born outside the country or who had spent their formative years outside Sri Lanka. Kandiah's chapter problematizes the securitized responses by the state to Tamil student activism from 2009. Drawing on social movement theory and critical ethnographic methodology, this chapter also considers how student activists responded to claims that protestors were "terrorists." Kandiah argues that rather than continuing to marginalize and criminalize a generation of Tamil activists, there is value in recognizing the meaningful collaborations that exist between student activists, analysts, and state actors in the context of Sri Lanka's fragile and ongoing transitional justice process.

Chapter 8, "#yosoy132: Indignation, Information and Pro-Democracy Activism in Mexico, 2011–2012," is by Lorna Zamora Robles. Drawing on auto-ethnographic material, on testimonies from students themselves and relevant literature, this chapter establishes how and why Mexican university students organized themselves during the #yosay123 movement. Robles focuses on the role of social media in the communication and mobilization strategies of students. She also considers the legacy of the #yosay123' (I am student 132). The movement emerged in 2012 when the Mexican presidential campaigns were met with a spontaneous eruption of protests by tens of thousands of university students who mobilized online using the hash tag #yosoy132. Their call went viral. They demanded, among other things, recognition of people's human rights and the democratization of the media. They did this while forging new ways of participating in politics. In this way, #yosoy132 challenged the stereotype of "youth as apathetic," as too privileged and as too self-centered to engage in politics. Robles also documents how this student action helped to open new spaces for collective action, for self-taught human rights education, for the development of skills had application for the defense of the right to political organization which continues ten years later.

Since the beginning of the twenty-first century, we have heard much public commentary and policy discussion in the global north about the aging population. Think tanks and government treasury experts have talked up the problems expected from this major demographic shift. Experts predict the number of people sixty-five and older will triple by mid-century, from 531 million in 2010 to around 1.5 billion in 2050. In the United States, for example, the population of older people is expected to more than double, from 41 to 86 million.

While this is happening in the Global North, paradoxically, the world's population is expected to increase by 2 billion from 7.7 billion at present to 9.7 billion in 2050. During this period, it is expected that children below age

5 will be outnumbered by those aged 65 or above. That is, while we witness an aging population in the Global North, in the Global South the opposite is happening—described in terms of a "youth bulge" (UN 2020; Cooper et al. 2019).

Given these demographic shifts of a "youth bulge" in the Global South and an overall increase in the world population due to high fertility rates, and as the chapters in this volume highlight, young people will become—even more so than they are now—major political players. Their influence in shaping the next few decades is assured—by virtue of their sheer numbers. This will be especially so in the Global South. Unlike older people, their influence will continue expanding across the twenty-first century. If the 1.2 billion young people, aged 15–24 years who account for one in every six people on earth were a demographic factor to be reckoned with in 2015, their demographic influence can only increase. In the 2020s, their numbers are expected to grow by 7 percent. By 2050, 30 percent of 15–24-year-olds in the world will be in sub-Saharan Africa up from 18 percent in 2020 (UN 2020). "Their numbers are expected to continue to grow, especially in the least developed regions" (Wickramanayake 2020).[5] Given this, we expect to see young people in the Global South exert an increasingly significant political effect.

If we understand this development politically, then the preoccupation with the aging population problem in the Global North can be understood as part of a desperate exercise on the part of neoliberal regimes to divert attention away from more basic political, existential challenges. Those immediate challenges include climate change, rapidly increasing inequality globally and domestically in many countries, stagnant economic growth in the advanced economies, massive technological disruption, and the rise of a new global economic and political hegemony in China. This is to say nothing of the dawning recognition that the last forty years have more than amply revealed the extent of the policy disaster initiated in the late 1970s by proponents of neoliberalism in the Global North. That catastrophe generated these problems, began when governments led by Thatcher (Britain), Regan (America), Hawke (Australia), Lange (New Zealand), Chirac (France), and Mulroney (Canada) moved to overturn policy practices that had generated decades of high growth and modest increases in social equality after 1945. As this volume demonstrates, many students and young people generally in the Global South have already worked this out.

NOTES

1. Volume 1: *When Students Protest: Secondary and High Schools*, Volume 2: *When Students Protest: Universities in the Global South*, Volume 3: *When Students Protest: Universities in the Global North.*

2. Other terminology includes "majority" and "minority" worlds because the majority of the population live in poorer, developing countries (mostly Global South), while the minority live in wealthier, more developed countries (mostly Global North).

3. The World Bank (2020) also has classifications according to "region," "income" and "lending," while the International Labour Organization (ILO 2020) uses both its own "regional groupings" (Africa, Americas, Arab States, Asia and the Pacific, Europe, and Central Asia), and "country groupings" (AL, APEC, ASEAN, AU, BRICS, CARICOM, ECOWAS, EU, G20, G7, LDC, MERCOSUR, OAS, OECD, SAARC, SADC). The United Nations (2020, 12) uses the terms "more developed regions" and "less developed regions."

4. Such insight is unlikely to be available through approaches that privilege more "evidence-based epistemology" and general positivist traditional forms of empirical inquiry typically carried out by outsiders distant from the lived experiences of participants.

5. Jayathma Wickramanayake (from Sri Lanka) was appointed the United Nations General-Secretary's Envoy on Youth in 2017 (when aged 26). In her "Workplan Vision Statement," we can read "Currently our world is home to 1.8 billion young people between the ages of 10 to 24, the largest generation of young people in its history. Close to 90 per cent of this youth population live in developing countries" (Wickramanayake 2020).

REFERENCES

Alcadipani, Rafael, Khan, Farzad Rafi, Gantman, Ernesto and Nkomo, Stella. 2012. Southern voices in management and organization knowledge. *Organization* 19(2): 131–143.

Bessant, Judith. 2021. *Making-Up People: Youth, Truth and Politics*. London and New York: Routledge.

Bessant, Judith, Pickard, Sarah and Watts, Rob. 2019. Translating Bourdieu. *Journal of Youth Studies* 23(1): 76–92. (https://doi.org/10.1080/13676261.2019.1702633)

Brandt, Willy. 1980. *North-South: A Programme for Survival. The Brandt Report*. Report of the Independent Commission on International Development Issues. Cambridge, MA: MIT Press.

Bühler-Niederberger, Doris and van Krieken, Robert. 2008. Persisting inequalities: Childhood between global influences and local traditions. *Childhood* 15(2): 147–155.

Connell, Raewyn. 2007. *Southern Theory: The Global Dynamics of Knowledge in Social Science*. Sydney: Allen and Unwin.

Cooper, Adam, Swartz, Sharlene and Mahali, Alude. 2019. Disentangled, decentred and democratised: Youth studies for the global South. *Journal of Youth Studies* 22(1): 29–45. (https://doi.org/10.1080/13676261.2018.1471199)

Fukuyama, Francis. 1992. *The End of History and the Last Man*. New York: The Free Press.

Furlong, Andy, ed. 2017. *Routledge Handbook of Youth and Young Adulthood.* Second edition. London and New York: Routledge.
Gale, Trevor. 2009. 'Towards a Southern Theory of Higher Education.' In *Preparing for Tomorrow Today: First Year in Higher Education Conference 2009.* Brisbane: Queensland University of Technology (QUT).
Gramsci, Antonio. 2006. *The Southern Question.* Toronto: Guernica Editions.
Heidegger, Martin. 1962. *Being and Time.* Translated by John Macquarrie and Edward Robinson. London: SCM Press.
International Labour Organization (ILO). 2020. 'Regions and countries.' (https://www.ilo.org/global/regions/lang—en/index.htm)
Jazeel, Tariq, and McFarlane, Colin. 2010. The limits of responsibility: A postcolonial politics of academic knowledge production. *Transactions of the Institute of British Geography* 35(1): 109–124.
Keim, Wiebke. 2011. Counterhegemonic currents and internationalization of sociology: Theoretical reflections and an empirical example. *International Sociology* 26(1): 123–145.
Marks, Michael. 2014. 'Metaphors of global inequality.' Paper prepared for the annual meeting of the Western Political Science Association Seattle, Washington, USA, 17–19 April. (https://pdfs.semanticscholar.org/330a/77ec03d4f56c4bf5ad5bd3fe76b88b8c74cf.pdf)
Meekosha, Helen. 2008. 'Contextualising disability: Developing southern/global theory.' Keynote Address 4th Biennial Disability Studies Conference, Lancaster University, UK, 2–4 September.
Meekosha, Helen. 2011. Decolonising disability: Thinking and acting globally. *Disability and Society* 26(6): 31–48.
Nilan, Pam. 2011. Youth sociology must cross cultures. *Youth Studies Australia* 30(3): 20–26.
Nilan, Pam and Feixa, Carlos, eds. 2006. *Global Youth? Hybrid Identities, Plural Worlds.* London and New York: Routledge.
Pickard, Sarah. 2019. *Politics, Protest and Young People.* London: Palgrave Macmillan.
Piketty, Thomas. 2020. *Capital and Ideology.* Cambridge, MA: Harvard University Press. Translated by Arthur Goldhammer.
Said, Edward. 1993. *Culture and Imperialism.* New York: Vintage.
Spivak Chakravorty, Gayatri. 1988. 'Can the subaltern speak?' In: *Marxism and the Interpretation of Culture*, edited by C. Nelson and G. Grossberg. Urbana: University of Illinois Press.
Steger, Manfred. 2017. *Globalization: A Very Short Introduction.* Fourth edition. Oxford: Oxford University Press.
Sukarieh, Mayssoun and Tannock, Stuart. 2008. In the best interests of youth or neoliberalism? The World Bank and the New Global Youth Empowerment Project. *Journal of Youth Studies* 11(3): 301–312.
Sukarieh, Mayssoun and Tannock, Stuart. 2011. The positivity imperative: A critical look at the 'new' youth development movement. *Journal of Youth Studies* 14(6): 675–691.

Sukarieh, Mayssoun and Tannock, Stuart. 2014. *Youth Rising: The Politics of Youth in the Global Economy*. London and New York: Routledge.

Sukarieh, Mayssoun and Tannock, Stuart. 2016. On the political economy of youth: A comment. *Journal of Youth Studies* 19(9): 1281–1289.

Sukarieh, Mayssoun and Tannock, Stuart. 2018. The global securitisation of youth. *Third World Quarterly* 39(5): 854–870.

Swartz, Sharlene, Cooper, Adam Cooper, Batan, Clarence and Camarena-Cordova, Rosa-Maria, eds. 2021 (forthcoming). *Oxford Handbook of Global South Youth Studies*. Oxford: Oxford University Press (OUP).

Tilly, Charles. 1986. *The Contentious French*. Cambridge, MA: Harvard University Press.

Tilly, Charles. 1995. *Popular Contention in Great Britain 1758–1934*. Cambridge: Cambridge University Press.

Todorov, Tzvetan. 1999. *The Conquest of America: The Question of the Other*. Oklahoma: University of Oklahoma. (Translated by Howard Richard).

United Nations (UN). 1951. *Measures for the Economic Development of Under-Developed Countries*. Report Group of Experts appointed by the Secretary-General of the United Nations. New York: United Nations.

United Nations (UN). 2020. *World Youth Report (WYR). Youth Social Entrepreneurship and the 2030 Agenda*. Department of Economic and Social Affairs (DESA). (https://www.un.org/development/desa/youth/wp-content/uploads/sites/21/2020/07/2020-World-Youth-Report-FULL-FINAL.pdf)

Vaughan-Williams, Nick. 2013. 'Cosmopolitanism and alternative modernities: Contest or renewal?' In *Cosmopolitanism and Diversity—Concepts, Practices and Policies in Education Abroad*, edited by A. Gristwood and M. Woolf. London: Occasional Publications No. 2, CAPA International Education.

Wallerstein, Immanuel. 2000. Globalization or the age of transition? A long-term view of the trajectory of the world system. *International Sociology* 15(2): 251–267.

Wickramanayake, Jayathma. 2020. United Nations General-Secretary's Envoy on Youth 'The envoy's workplan: Vision statement.' (https://www.un.org/youthenvoy/workplan)

World Bank. 2020. 'World Bank country and lending groups.' Data. (https://datahelpdesk.worldbank.org/knowledgebase/articles/906519-world-bank-country-and-lending-groups)

Chapter 2

Breaking Routines toward Conservatism?

The 2013 Protests in Brazil

Enzo Bello, Gustavo Capela, and Rene José Keller

In June 2013, routine life was abruptly interrupted in Brazil when millions of people took the streets—in a decentralized manner throughout every major city—during the entire month. To those who lived that moment, in part due to intensity of the protests, and in part due to its duration, it seemed, smelled, and sounded as if a major political transformation were coming. In what was perhaps the most emblematic moment of that hope, protesters occupied the building that houses the Brazilian National Congress, in Brasilia, on June 17. That image—of tens of thousands of people charging and taking over an institutional branch of government—seemed to recall what had happened in the streets of Madrid, Tahrir Square, and it inserted itself, of course, in a long tradition of protesters in the history of Brazil as well as in world history. Naturally, these statements sound exaggerated—as they should—but that is what many felt at the time.

Perhaps what best illustrates this overwhelming feeling that the winds of radical change had arrived in Brazil is the slogan that took over the protests. It read: "the Giant has awoken." It was meant to reference: (1) the enormous size of Brazil; (2) its population of 200 million people; (3) the surprising amount of people on the streets; and, symptomatically, we could say that (4) an excluded majority that had grown tired of silent consent. The uprisings were so substantial and constant that schools, offices, and even entertainment venues had to close down. It seemed as though no one did anything else during that month in 2013. Nothing else was on the news despite the Federation of International Football Association's (FIFA) Confederation Cup taking place at the time in Brazil.

Since those turbulent moments of June 2013, Brazil saw the impeachment of its first woman president in 2015, the rise of a far-right that is racist, sexist, and xenophobic during that same period and, finally, the election of its best representative in Jair Bolsonaro in 2018. How did that happen? How did Brazil go from these protests in 2013 to an overly conservative government in just five years? Were the protests already in the name of that far-right agenda? Were they already xenophobic, homophobic, sexist, and racist?

Although the answer is complex, we must begin by saying that no, the protests were not conservative in character. On the contrary, the protests started with young people who wanted more democracy; who wanted more and better public services; who, in light of the abundant expenditure made by the Brazilian government to host the FIFA World Cup, requested that the same seriousness directed toward a football tournament be granted to education, health, and public safety.

However, things changed along the way. The protests took a turn that would, in our view, mold how Brazilian politics has developed since then. By saying this, however, we do not mean that these protests were the only relevant factor in determining what came after. Like any critical moment, these protests revealed a lot of the undercurrents that were present then and are still present now in Brazilian politics. Our overall thesis is that June 2013 is a relevant phenomenon to study because it broke the plain of normality, opened up a sense of new possibilities and intensified ideas of political resignification, if only for a moment. It exposed a crisis, a fissure in the social formation, and, in so doing, disclosed how different sectors of Brazilian society struggle for hegemony.

WHERE WE BEGIN

It is always hard to pinpoint exactly where or when something starts because the specific place or moment that is chosen is often overdetermined by so many other events and moments that the choice seems nothing less than arbitrary. With that in mind, we begin with an overall picture of the context in which June 2013 kicked off in Brazil.

There are four significant factors that we think help understand the conditions that made June 2013 possible. All of these factors point to situations that, in some form or another, broke routines, tilted normality, and, in so being, made more visible, or legible, certain demands for change.

The first factor was the political climate of the world at that time. In 2013, the world was in turmoil due to a financial crisis in 2008, and felt what seemed like winds of change due to the mobilization of peoples in the Middle East (the now-called Arab Spring), as well as the uprising of young people in places like Spain and the United States (see Pickard and Bessant 2017). These events pointed to something new, to a possible change, to a younger generation that could perhaps mold a different kind of world system (Pickard and Bessant 2017; Gerbaudo 2017; Pickard 2019).

The second factor has to do with the specific political history of Brazil, where the Worker's Party (PT—*Partido dos Trabalhadores*) came into power in 2003, with the first ever factory worker elected as president. Luiz Inácio Lula da Silva, hereafter just "Lula," was the president that promised to rule for the poor due to his own working-class background. Somewhat keeping with his promise, Lula was responsible for a great number of policies that benefited the lower classes (Almeida 2004) but did so through what several Brazilian social scientists have called "inclusion through consumption" (Grzybowski 2013; Neri 2008; Dagnino 2006; Bello et al. 2014). Starting in 2006, when a graft scandal that involved his party—the Worker's Party (PT—*Partido dos Trabalhadores*)—broke, he started to look more and more like a typical bourgeois politician (one whose interest trumps the working class's demands and desires). More importantly, this party (the PT) had represented the hope of many Brazilians after the military dictatorship[1] due to its message and its mechanisms of participation. The corruption scandals attacked not only the politicians of the PT but also the dreams of many Brazilians.

The third factor involves the selection made by FIFA in 2007 and the one made by the International Olympic Committee in 2009. Both decided that Brazil would host massive international sporting events (Men's World Cup in 2014, Rio Olympic Games in 2016) and, in so doing, would need to build stadiums, venues, and other infrastructure required. These selections were part of the Worker's Party idea of a "new Brazil": one that would be a powerful global player. However, in a country where 50 percent of the population does not have proper sewage systems, where illiteracy is still an issue and where the ruling party was seen as corrupt, the hosting of these large sporting events seemed like a political distraction from more pressing issues.

Finally, tying together the previous three, and also the factor that is most immediate to the commencement of the protests, was a raise in the bus fares in some of the largest cities of Brazil. The increase, originally planned to be implemented in January 2013, was pushed back a couple of months to help the federal government maintain the inflation target established by the Central Bank. To better understand the political relevance of this, we would have to delve into how the Worker's Party (*Partido dos Trabalhadores*) tried to distribute wealth without confronting the logic of austerity or the macroeconomic goals of primary surplus—something we have done elsewhere (Bello et al. 2014)—but here it is enough to point out that the Worker's Party (*Partido dos Trabalhadores*) method of governance was based on a type of conciliation that, according to Marcos Nobre (2013), mixed technocratic, expert, top-down decisions with pragmatic-political agreements. The latter were made with and within the political caste and the former by those who had access to elite educational institutions leading to what he (Nobre) called low intensity democracy.

It is within this context that a massive uprising appears. Due to its multiple origins and complex interweavings, it is an episode that speaks different languages and spreads into different social spheres. To gauge just how it developed, we need to examine the facts.

WHAT HAPPENED? PHASE 1

Initially, protests took place in São Paulo, where thousands of young people (mostly students) took the streets against an increase of 20 cents in the price of bus fares. Importantly, protests are not uncommon to the Brazilian political sphere. As there is a long history of social movements in the country, the staging of marches and other formats of protests are a common occurrence. At that time, it was just another march, as so many others before it. These protests were organized by Movimento Passe Livre (MPL)—the Free Fare Movement—a group of students who had known since January of that same year that the fare would go up, started to organize around bus and metro stations in the six months prior to June.

That build-up made it possible for MPL to put around 6,000 students on the streets of Avenida Paulista[2] on June 6 and 7, 2013. The idea of the protests was to overturn the increase in fares, but, as some of the leaders of the movement told us during and after the protests, they did not expect to be successful immediately. They knew that in order to defeat the government, they would have to be persistent, leading them to call for another protest on June 11. These became violent and authorities qualified the protester's acts as "vandalism." Not only the police, but Fernando Haddad, the Worker's Party (PT) young mayor of São Paulo, also corroborated the thesis of "vandals" taking the streets and destroying property. Haddad had also served as Lula's minister of education and many viewed him as sensitive to "social justice" causes. Not only did he express disgust against the protesters, but, in unison with the governor of the state, Geraldo Alckmin (leader of the conservative Brazilian Social Democracy Party—Partido Social Democrata Brasileiro), he supported the actions of the police force, who had been violent in trying to prevent the march from happening.

Keeping with their relentless strategy, one day after the violent clash with the police, MPL called for another protest on June 13. In response, the police spoke through the press to advise people against attending, because, in the police's words, "protesters would not feel at home on the streets."

On the same day, MPL put out a call for protests, Arnaldo Jabor[3] (2013b), one of the more qualified spokespersons of Brazil's largest communication conglomerate used his platform on primetime TV to express his opinion on the matter:

> The majority of the protesters are children. Children of the middle class. There were no poor people complaining about an increase of 20 cents in the bus fares. The actual poor people at the protests were the policemen. And they were the ones who had stones thrown at them, they are the ones who have to face that with a bad salary.

Jabor concluded his commentary by pointing out what he saw as a "historic obsolescence" of the methods used by protesters: "it is a violent caricature, a caricature of socialism from the 1950s. A socialism that the old left-wing still defends here in Brazil. If they were honest about their demands," Jabor went on, "these middle-class rebels would say that it is not about the 20 cents."

That last sentence ("it is not about the 20 cents") would later become a slogan of the movement. Protesters all over Brazil started saying that it was, in fact, about the 20 cents—as well as other things. Jabor did not anticipate (as no one did) what would become of the movement. The day after his appearance on television, São Paulo became the stage of a vicious (and televised) confrontation between protesters and the police. Journalists were hurt by the dozens and 240 people were detained by the police.[4]

In an unpredictable turn of events, the brutal violence used by the military police of the state of São Paulo lead to general indignation and transformed the nature and dimension of the protests. Immediately following the police violence in São Paulo, large numbers of unknown and mostly depoliticized people started using Facebook calling for protests "in solidarity" with what had happened with the "Free Fare Movement" (MPL) in São Paulo. What seemed like a naive response at the time, took on a life of its own. In less than an hour, multiple Facebook events in Brasilia, for example, had more than 15,000 people "attending."

In hindsight and taking into account what was experienced by all three of us during the protests, it seems that Jabor's words might have made legible a form of solidarity among young people. The encounter between his televised dismissal and the televised violence seemed to produce it and spread from São Paulo to the rest of the country. The Facebook events created constantly called for "solidarity" with MPL and, because Jabor had used the terms "middle class" and "children" to discredit the protesters, the rhetoric of organizers invoked the youth's and the middle class's right to protest. Students were within their rights to march on the streets, they said.

It is only through this unpredictable expansion that the protests of June 2013 became so relevant. Herein lies two paradoxes that will be explored as we continue to analyze the process. First, what started as a localized protest organized by a social movement through pamphlets and word of mouth was expanded by the bourgeois media as it tried to denounce the protesters; second, with its escalation, its massification, what began as a protest with very clear objectives, in a very specific city, became an arena for diffused, dispersed, abstract, and imprecise demands. What was initially about the increase in bus fares (the 20 cents) became about better public health care, better public education, against police brutality and eventually against corruption, against the government, and against political parties.

Again paradoxically, when we spoke of June 2013 as a process that "broke the plain of normality," we were speaking of this moment, of the moment when it expanded, when it was more diffuse, when it had already been produced by an articulation of what a social movement had planned and done, the reaction to those acts by the police, the intervention by mass media and political actors and the organization of protests by individuals on social media. This expansion created something else, something new, something unknown, unseen, untamable. It was leaderless, it had no strict policy on participation and it brought young people to the streets that had not been politically active before, much like was the case with protests in other places around the world (Castells 2013; Graeber 2014; Pickard and Bessant 2017).

GROWING PAINS—DIFFICULTIES OF A BROADER POLITICS

Once the protests grew in scale, it did not take long before other, more imprecise and general demands, made their way onto the streets. A desire for social transformation was evident, engaging people in demands for what they believed "change" would entail: better public health care system, safety, education, less corruption, a better political system, and so on. The police violence exerted by the Military Police of São Paulo seems to have violently opened a wound, or, as Jodi Dean would have it, opened "the gap of the political" (Dean 2018, 255).

Once a gap is opened, it can either expand its borders and, in doing so, intensify the crisis that started it, or it can retract in order to do away with the possible problems that expanding it entails. What would it mean to continue to question the violence of the state in a place like Brazil? Or, in the context of the large international sporting events that were to happen, with its consequent dislocation of impoverished communities to build stadiums and venues, what would it mean to question the political system that benefits those with more money? How could problems such as these be effectively solved? These and other questions were a constant during this second phase of June 2013. Assemblies were held in various cities to discuss what could be done, what a political reform could look like, what a different political economy could be like and so forth. What the protests gained in imagination, they lost in concreteness, however. There were a lot of questions, a great amount of indignation, but not as many concrete objectives. People usually spoke of a desire for more democracy, for an expansion of public services, but these demands depended more on the elected officials than the overturning of the raise in the bus fares. Whereas the latter requires one act (cancel the price raise), the former demands a string of actions that, in their turn, demand social pressures that are more lasting. An extensive and radical political reform, for example, would require more energy.

This difficulty, a difficulty that any larger, broader, demand entails, was perhaps more intense because of how activists were brought together in this second phase. Whereas MPL—the Free Fare Movement—is a group that meets in person, that has structures in place, has a clear membership policy, and a history of existence since 2005, the protesters of this second phase of June 2013 had none of that. Participants got together by Facebook events, Facebook groups, or other virtual media. This became one of the hardest issues to deal with. Not only did they need to create intense and lasting bonds to obtain "more democracy, more public services, a political reform" and so on, there was also a question of how one could bring together the thousands of people on the Internet to meet in person. The organization, or lack of organization, through the Internet, made the translation of people's demands from the virtual to the "physical" sphere difficult. It was one thing to go to the streets, where people could protest whatever they wanted (one could see a poster asking for more education and, beside it, one that clamored for a military intervention), but it was a completely different task to accumulate political will toward a specific agenda.

David Harvey argues (2012, 118) that movements like these are a product of a specific phase of capitalism (i.e., financial-technological-communicational) in which space and time are reconfigured through continuous flows of information, experiences, and truth regimes. The movements are, thus, interpellated (Althusser 2014, 264) and constituted as such by the same informational flows and regimes that are paramount to the structure and functioning of capitalism. For him, Facebook is not just used as a simple instrument, as a neutral tool, but it interpellates subjects, constructing them in a specific manner. These movements, in his account, experience volatility in respect to their growth, but also decay—and are easily controlled and absorbed by dominant practices of capitalism because they are constituted by the very structure they seem to question.

Another way to look at it—without dismissing Harvey's rendering of what is typical in movements constituted through and by social media—is to insist on the idea of a gap that is opened—and, with it, to understand, for example, with Althusser, that ruptures are created by contradictions that are overdetermined (2005, 113). What he means by that is that situations and subjects are constituted by an "accumulation of effective determinations." Social media and structural problems play a part, yes, but there are other factors, other determinations, that should be understood as well. Not everything is (or can be) controlled by capital or large conglomerates, even though that is the tendency, due to the logic imposed on us by a system as large and complex as capitalism. What transpired after the massification of the protests leads us to believe that the streets of Brazil were a space of opened dispute—brought on by a chaotic intervention of millions of Brazilians—and what prevailed has more to do with the means actors had for producing political alternatives than the preconditioned aspects that constituted the political subjects in the political arena.

JUNE'S PHASE 2: TRACES OF CONSERVATISM

As we said, it was the second phase of June 2013 that ruptured broke routines and ruptured normality of life in Brazil. It was only then that what began as usual protests by 5,000 or 6,000 students took an unexpected turn and amplified its potency as well as its reach. The country seemed like it had stopped in order to look at these protests whose goals no one could really understand. Not even its participants. On one of the largest protests in Rio, while walking among tens of thousands of people we spotted an individual with a sign that read "Ground beef 9.99." We could not tell if he was protesting about the price of meat, if he was a butcher, if he simply took the first sign he saw or if it was merely making a joke. In a way, this was the atmosphere that made the large movement welcoming. It seemed like people could protest whatever they wanted. It seemed like anything fitted within those protests.

However, that was not entirely true. One of the important paths that the protest took was to stand against political parties. People who went to the protests wearing shirts or bearing banners of parties were asked to leave and sometimes even violently attacked. The shift in June was, therefore, not merely one that gained in abstraction, but it also questioned certain forms of organization and not others.

This type of restrictive action has a long-standing tradition in Brazil, especially among the middle class (Dreyfus 1981, 291). Dreyfus (1981, 292–295) narrates important moments prior to the military coup in 1964 where a significant part of the middle class in Brazil took the streets in order to protest against corruption and in favor of the traditional moral values of society. At that moment in time, the American ambassador in Brazil—who was part of the coup—made sure to reaffirm that the protests were not of working-class character, but made up of mostly middle-class women (Dreyfus 1981, 297–298).

This historical tendency of the middle class in Brazil helps explain the shift that not only made demands more abstract but also took a turn toward morality. The stance against corruption, as abstract as it was, began reasserting some sense of cleanliness and traditional values that should be upheld by the political elite.

Some will argue (Braga 2013, 82) that it was not the middle class that took the streets in the second phase of June 2013, but a collection of diverse precarious workers. With Singer (2013), however—and based on the empirical research he used to make his statements—we understand that although June did harbor precarious workers in its ranks, it was hegemonized by a middle-class ethos.

What we mean by the middle-class ethos is that, contrary to what Braga supposes, the June protests did not refer to the conditions of the workplace or question, directly, the structure of capitalism (even though, of course, that was in the background of all the indignation). What we saw was a general discontent and a process that distanced itself from the idea of a "working-class" or a political subject that is part of an overwhelming structure and, therefore, need to lose their shackles. As is typical of the middle class (Firmino 2017), there is an attempt to distance themselves from everything that is branded as "working class"—to mark their difference.

Nevertheless, Braga is correct in pointing out the presence of precarious workers even though the progress of this second phase of June 2013 was eventually hegemonized by the middle class. As we stated before, June was disputed by various sectors of society and, eventually, what prevailed (at least in June) was an anti-party (in reality an anti-politics) agenda.

This agenda is what leads to the void in terms of political representation. If people are against political parties in a democracy, what could represent them?

FROM ANTI-POLITICS TO CONSERVATIVE POLITICS: THE NOVELTY OF A YOUTH CONSERVATIVE MOVEMENT

Up until June 2013, the student movement in Brazil was understood to be a place of left-wing politics. This does not mean that society in general held left-wing views, but that the organized mass of students generally sided with socialists, social democrats, and communists. One of the novelties of June was that this circumstance changed.

Two of the most important political facts that followed June 2013 stem directly from it. The first was a nationwide occupation of public high schools by students, between 2015 and 2016, who demanded better conditions for teachers and education in general. This was a process hegemonized by the left-wing agenda (e.g., more and better public services) and extremely criticized by right-wing conservative groups. The second was the impeachment of then-president Dilma Rousseff, which was led by a group of students who began their activities during June 2013. The name they use for their movement (MBL) is actually a play on words on the Free Fare Movement's name, which, as we mentioned, is MPL. While MPL stands for Free Fare, MBL stands for a "Free Brazil." In trying to disrupt the logic of what should be "free," these students asserted the importance of a free market, of privatization and of the end of leftist political parties as the solution to Brazil's problems. Brazil should be free from political intervention in the market, from victim-based politics and from "communists," in their rhetoric.

The gap we referenced earlier as being opened by June 2013, is one that challenged the party model, that questioned the role of professional politicians, that insisted on the necessity of a new generation in power. And it bred MBL—*Movimento Brasil Livre*—the Free Brazil Movement.

The tactics used by the MBL were effective in attracting students to commit to their conservative guidelines for a couple of reasons. Some were already stated (lack of trust in those in power, a crisis of the Worker's Party etc.), and others were due to a special attention to organizing through the Internet. As we stated earlier, the difficulty to organize and to produce social bonds that would be capable of intensifying political bonds among those that were on the streets in 2013 was felt by most protesters. And the largest difficulty was due to the complicated relationship between the virtual sphere and the physical space of politics. MBL seemed to solve that problem. There was a massive adherence of students, mainly those from middle and upper classes, because this was a movement that did not need, as they stated (Gobbi 2016), traditional forms of organization. The Internet allowed them to use the funds they received from *think tanks* (mostly established in the United States) (Gobbi 2016) to push a "fun" and "bold" form of neoliberal rationale. Free market, free trade, privatization of public services all became "cool" and "fun" through performative denunciation on the Internet, "trolling" politicians—personal attacks, humiliating videos, physical confrontation of political adversaries became a constant—as well as the creation of memes carrying controversial themes.

The leaders of this "anti-establishment," "anti-politics," movement not only pushed forward the protests that culminated in the ousting of then-president

Dilma Rousseff, but also began working for the most conservative parties of Brazil. In 2016, during the municipal elections, some of their leaders ran successful campaigns for the legislative branches through these ultraconservative parties. In 2018, the same students who founded MBL in 2013 endorsed the campaign of the ultraconservative now-president Jair Bolsonaro.[5]

How Do We Come to Terms with June 2013? Theoretical Components

In an article about a shopping frenzy that occurred on a day that traditionally leftist organizations (such as Labor Unions) had called for strikes in Portugal, Maria Jose de Abreu depicts different crowds in distinct turmoil to question the temporality of politics. Just like the protesters of June 2013 in Brazil, shoppers in Portugal were affected by a wave of calls and messages on Facebook that went viral in a very short period of time. Borrowing from de Abreu's description of how the sale at Pingo Doce spread, we could say that "From mouth to mouth, medium to medium, news of the [protests] spread to all corners of [Brazil] and beyond" (De Abreu 2018).

By examining the medium that at once produces and conditions the message even as the message produces and conditions the medium, De Abreu shows how the different flows of desire can be captured by capital and, in turn, can challenge its logic. What is this desire, how is it produced, what does it produce?

When Gustave LeBon says that "crowds are only powerful for destruction" (LeBon 2007), he might be right in the sense that George Bataille understands human desire—a continuous demand for excess, expenditure and, finally, destruction (Bataille 1997). This crowd, this momentous union of people we were a part of in June 2013, seemed to expand on that notion of excess by reproducing some of Brazil's typical activities during carnival. If these protests did in fact express a desire for expenditure, excess, and destruction, it was done with flirting, singing, dancing. Like an important ritual perhaps, the fun was had, but in a very serious tone, if that could at all be imagined.

Yet, what is most interesting about these different flows of desire and their different concentration is the fact that in De Abreu's story, since the people did not follow the expected stream by the leftist protesters, it made it possible for her to expand on a notion of impasse. As she understands, the idea of crisis has become overwhelmingly used by people—both in power and against it—to explain the problems of sociality. So much so that it has become a stumbling block for actually solving anything. To her, crisis has become an idiom that expands on exploitation due to its normalization.

De Abreu makes the point that although the word "crisis" brings about a notion of emergency, what it does in fact is hide the actual urgencies.

In June 2013, Brazil's protesters were on the street against what they saw as a "crisis" of representation. A "crisis" of the traditional structures of politics. "Crisis" in Brazil, like in Portugal, was a term used both by the powerful and the crowds. With De Abreu, one wonders how her argument for the use of "impasse" as a method could expand on the fragments that those protests have left Brazil with. What exactly is the potentiality of impasse?

Impasse, in De Abreu's work, is an active gesture of inquiry that renders visible articulations and concealed elements buried underneath, or, to say it plainly, it is a call for more questions and less answers, more openings and less closure, more dwelling, less moving on. Well, is that possible within the temporality of politics?

Alain Badiou (2002) offers a few insights that are helpful in this situation because temporality is, for him, an important aspect of determining if an event is, in fact, a political one. For him, a political event is one which produces possibilities that were once invisible, impossible, and, thus, creates an idea that is capable of engaging people in such a manner that they (the people in the event) are reconfigured, re-subjectified capable of opening new possibilities. The disruption caused by this "political event," thus, can only be read, can only be understood, in its aftermath. It is only then that one is able to recognize and appreciate the new truths that were bred in the process.

As De Abreu poses, then, there is a specific temporality within politics that renders the coexistence of different histories, different paths and different flows of people, capital, structures visible. It is within politics, then, that one must impose temporality of impasse, a pause, a slowing down, to be able to produce new possibilities.

Looking at it from Badiou's lenses, the new truths that are linked to the political events depend on the loyal *adhesion* of the subject to that event, or, in other words, it creates a rupture, a gap, whereby what has become, what "is" after the event is now the truth. And what came before is now false. The subject is constituted in that new truth as much as the event is produced by this surging subjectivity. They are co-constitutive, just as the medium and the subjects are in DeAbreu's rendering: there is a dialectical relationship between what constitutes the subject and the subject itself, between its connection to the event and their separation.

Herein lies, then, the question of whether or not June 2013 was able to produce new truths, if it was able to linger on impasses, or if it "dessignified" the possible political advances, as Žižek (2014, 180) would have it?

In using Badiou's framework, the answer seems straightforward. For him, a political event would have to reorganize the structures of society, its functioning, its quotidian existence. June 2013 did not go so far. It opened wounds and gaps that seem to still be opened, but the forms of life continue the same, we would say.

However, one could take some fragments of Badiou's conception of the event to, as De Abreu proposes, insert questions within such rigid affirmations. Badiou says that a political event inaugurates or puts forth a new historicity because it reframes the interpretation of facts that were previous to it (to the political event). In that sense, June 2013 is perhaps still pulsating, still writing, new interpretations. Therefore, while as of now we cannot really propose that it constituted new truths, its potential seems to live on.

Going even further, the election of Bolsonaro, the rise of this extreme right in Brazil, as well as the creation of a conservative student movement are important factors that, if not created by June 2013, were amalgamated because of it. Are not political events those that bring together different flows and, due to improbable and unpredictable circumstances, produce new subjects? The overriding trope of June proclaimed that *the giant had woken up*. In a way, it seems to reference a new, empowered, speaking, subject. A new political subject that had woken up, that had the veils of ignorance taken away from it. This "giant" was, supposedly, a new, capable, conscious, voice that would expel all the "signifieds" that had been struggling vainly to find adequate signifiers.

Our view is that this 'new' subject is at the forefront of the conservative agenda in Brazil. The newest party in the Brazilian political arena—a party that considers itself neoliberal—calls itself "New": the New Party. They use this image of something that was bred, something that was created, that will extract the old structures in place. But what are these old structures and what are the new ones, we could ask? Their answer would probably give us good insight into the type of subject that prevailed after this process that began with students, took the streets with millions, ousted a president and, eventually, elected Jair Bolsonaro. To them, the "new" is the market, the "old" is anything that questions it, making us question if a political event can produce new truths that simply reiterate old views in new formats.

CONCLUSION

In June 2013, the protests begin due to a raise in the bus fares. Something that did not only affect students and young people but affected them in a way that became more significant than other sectors. First, because in Brazil they are constantly interpellated as relevant political actors who can and should stand against the government. Second, because a specific social movement, MPL, was effectively engaging young people on the streets, in schools, at metro stations, in order to organize them and to make them feel like the raise would affect them more so than anyone. Lastly, because the first gigantic increase in numbers that happened in the protests was done through social media and through the social media of young people. As Castells explains, the logic of social media networks is partly[6] to identify people whose interests, personal networks, and culture, in some way, shape or form, overlap. So, it would make sense that students and the young people of Brazil were not only the ones who began the protest, but also the overwhelming majority of protesters.

Having said that, we began this chapter invoking the broken routines due to the overwhelming power of the protests. The power of any crowd, especially of a politically engaged crowd, is to interrupt normality, to impose new temporalities. The young people that took the streets in June 2013 did that: they made the whole country stop, rearrange itself, reorganize its functioning if only just for a month. What we have tried to expose in these few pages are the complex networks and disputes in play before, during, and after that episodic month. We argued that the Journeys of June 2013 were not left-wing or right-wing movement, per se, but that there were struggles within the process and consequent (re)signification by different actors.

As we have said, when a gap is opened, when a rupture breaks apart normality, it is possible to intensify the ruptures, to escalate the structural conflicts, or to retrocede and conserve the status quo. The symptoms that have remained have pointed to a continuous rise in conservatism, and the extreme right-wing agenda of now-president Jair Bolsonaro. This thread, of course, is not bred exclusively from June, but stems from multiple sources: we highlight, in the case of Brazil, the frustration with the Worker's Party combined with the active role of traditional media groups (Castells 2009) and a general crisis of liberal institutions across the globe (Gerbaudo 2017).

The recent Brazilian conjuncture shows that students are also not organized in the same way as they used to be in the past. The advent of social media was essential to these and other transformations (Veronese and Capela 2017). It has had an effect on the methods of organization and the effective action of student groups. Notwithstanding, recently it was once again the students who led a protest against the measures of the right-wing government, demonstrating the continuous struggles within the student movement in general.

In our view, as June 2013 still lingers on the mind of every person that is politically active in Brazil, we are left wondering how much different sectors have learned from it, mystified it, or taken it for granted.

NOTES

1. Brazil was ruled by a US-backed military dictatorial regime from 1964 to 1985.
2. The most famous street in the financial center of São Paulo, Brazil.

3. Arnaldo Jabor is an internationally renowned Brazilian journalist. During the 1990s, he began acting as a political commentator on the radio and television at *Rede Globo*, the largest newsgroup of Brazil. Despite the fact that in his youth he was close to the Brazilian Communist Party (*Partido Comunista Brasileiro*—PCB), Jabor spoke out against social policies, racial quotas and other issues that were part of the Worker's Party agenda (2003–2016).

4. The numbers can be viewed here: (https://noticias.uol.com.br/cotidiano/ultimas-noticias/2013/06/13/em-dia-de-maior-repressao-da-pm-ato-em-sp-termina-com-jornalistas-feridos-e-mais-de-60-detidos.htm)

5. Jair Bolsonaro is a former military captain from the Brazilian Army (1973–1988). He was forcibly retired because of a controversial administrative process that investigated his responsibility in the attempts to bomb army headquarters in the state of Rio de Janeiro, to which he confessed (Veja 2017). Born in the state of São Paulo, Bolsonaro was councilor of the city of Rio de Janeiro (1989-1991) and federal deputy (1991–2018) by the state of Rio de Janeiro. He was elected on a corporativist platform with ultraconservative guidelines and hate speech, mainly through prejudice against gays, women, and black people. He also supported the civil-military-entrepreneurial dictatorship (1964–1985) and its leaders, like the confessed torturer and former Colonel Carlos Alberto Brilhante Ustra. Three of Bolsonaro's five sons have been elected to the Parliament in public mandates of city councilor, state deputy, federal deputy, and senator. After the impeachment of Dilma Rousseff in 2016, Bolsonaro began to present himself as a representative of the so-called "new politics" and an alternative to the corruption attributed to the center left-wing PT governments. After his affiliation to 8 right-wing political parties, he got into PSL—*Partido Social Liberal* (Social Liberal Party)—in 2018, specifically to run for president, catalyzing ancient and new right-wing supporters: those of customs and those of market economics.

6. It is not limited to this function, but it does work within this logic.

REFERENCES

Almeida, Maria Hermínia Tavares de. 2004. 'A política social no Governo Lula.' *Novos Estudos—CEBRAP* 70: 7–17.

Badiou, Alain. 2012. *A Hipótese Comunista*. São Paulo: Boitempo. [2015. *The Communist Hypothesis*. London: Verso].

Bello, Enzo, Rene José Keller, and Renata Piroli Mascarello. 2014. 'Brazil's 'New middle class' and the effectiveness of social rights through consumption: A dialectic of inclusion and exclusion.' *Birkbeck Law Review* 2: 129–145. http://www.bbklr.org/uploads/1/4/5/4/14547218/bbklr-2.1_ecopy.pdf.

Braga, Ruy. 2013. 'Sob a sombra do precariado.' In *Cidades Rebeldes*, edited by Ermínia Maricato et al., 45–51. São Paulo: Boitempo.

De Abreu, Maria Jose. 2018. 'May day supermarket: Crisis, impasse, medium.' *Critical Inquiry* 44(4): 745–765.

Dean, Jodi. 2018. *Crowds and Party*. New York: Verso.

Firmino, Gustavo Casasanta. 2017. 'Classes Médias e Manifestações pró-*impeachment* na cidade de São Paulo: uma análise dos movimentos e manifestantes.' *Revista de Ciências Sociais* 47: 209–227.

Gerbaudo, Paolo. 2017. *Mask and the Flag: Populism, Citizenism and Global Protest.* Oxoford: Oxford University Press.

Grzybowski, Candido. 2013. 'Que Brasil Estamos Construindo?' In *A Nova Classe Média no Brasil Como Conceito e Projeto Político*, edited by Dawid D. Bartelt, 97. Rio de Janeiro: Fundação Heinrich Böll.

Harvey, David. 2012. *Rebel Cities: From the Right to the City to Urban Revolution.* London/New York: Verso.

Jabor, Arnaldo. 2013a. 'Comentário de Arnaldo Jabor realizado em 17 de jun. 2013.' *Rádio Cbn*, 17 June 2013. http://cbn.globoradio.globo.com/comentaristas/arnaldo-jabor/2013/06/17/AMIGOS-EU-ERREI-E-MUITO-MAIS-DO-QUE-20-CENTAVOS.htm. Acesso em 10 de out. 2018.

Jabor, Arnaldo. 2013b. 'Comentário de Arnaldo Jabor no Jornal Nacional.' *Jornal Nacional*, 18 June 2013. https://www.youtube.com/watch?v=luLzhtSYWC4/.

LeBon, Gustav. 2007. *The Crowd a Study of the Popular Mind.* Eastbourne: Gardners Books.

Neri, Marcelo. 2008. *A Nova Classe Média.* Rio de Janeiro: FGV.

Pickard, Sarah. 2019. *Politics, Protest and Young People.* London: Palgrave Macmillan.

Pickard, Sarah and Bessant, Judith (eds). 2017. *Young People Re-Generating Politics in Times of Crises.* London: Palgrave Macmillan.

Singer, André. 2013. 'Brasil, junho de 2013: classes e ideologias cruzadas.' *Novos Estudos-CEBRAP* 97: 23–40.

Veja. 'O artigo em VEJA e a prisão de Bolsonaro nos anos 1980.' *Redação—Veja*, 15 May 2017. https://veja.abril.com.br/blog/reveja/o-artigo-em-veja-e-a-prisao-de-bolsonaro-nos-anos-1980/.

Veronese, Alexandre and Capela, Gustavo Moreira. 2017. 'Petições em linha e ação política: aplicações de comunicação ou de participação política?' *Cadernos Adenauer* 18(1): 35–57.

Žižek, Slavoj. 2014. *Event: A Philosophical Journey Through a Concept.* Harmondsworth: Penguin.

Chapter 3

The Student Movement in Chile

Normalizing Protest and Opening Up Political Space

Sofia Donoso and Nicolás Somma

INTRODUCTION

In early May 2019, the Federación de Estudiantes de la Universidad de Chile (The Federation of Students of the University of Chile), historically the backbone of the country's student movement, announced that it had not reached the minimum quorum required to validate its internal elections. A transitory executive board was, therefore, to be established. The failure to renew the Federación de Estudiantes de la Universidad de Chile leadership contrasted sharply with the fervor and engagement that characterized the student movement just a few years earlier. In 2011, hundreds of thousands of students across the country marched and called for free, public quality education. The lack of response by the government at the time, a center-right coalition presided by Sebastián Piñera, only fueled protest further. As the year ended, the students' petition had expanded to include not only an overhaul of the education system, but also a tax reform to finance the proposed changes, and a change of the country's constitution to make the reforms politically viable. The student movement had spurred a national debate on the pending reforms since the transition to democracy twenty years earlier. Importantly, the movement received the support of public opinion. Public surveys showed how education increased as a priority among Chileans. They also indicated that the vast array of repertoires of action deployed by the student movement—marches, flash mobs, occupations, among others—were considered legitimate means of protests.

In the parliamentary election that followed the 2011 student protest wave, some of the former leaders decided to dispute power in the electoral arena and succeeded. The movement's demands also gained traction as the incoming government, presided by Michelle Bachelet from the Socialist Party, included many of the issues raised by the students in an ambitious policy agenda. This entailed almost thirty bills, covering areas such as primary, secondary, and tertiary education, improvements to the Teachers' Statute, and the most important tax reform since 1990 to finance the proposed education reforms. Pushing for the overhaul of the education system and its neoliberal formulation, students continued to mobilize. In parallel, former student leaders in Parliament also pressed for the advancement of the education agenda.

After many years of depoliticization and demobilization of civil society actors, the student movement significantly contributed to the normalization of protests in Chile. In doing so, it played a central role in both questioning the governance formula that has dominated politics since the reinstatement of democracy and pushing for political reforms that can deepen democracy. In this effort, other social movements joined the students, placing issues such as pensions, the environment, sexual violence and gender discrimination, among others, at the top of the policy agenda. As a result, during the last decade Chileans have become accustomed to the rise of social movements that articulate extant discontent with issues insufficiently addressed by the traditional political parties.

What has been the role of the student movement in normalizing protest and reshaping the content and terms of politics in post-transition Chile? This chapter describes this process drawing on interview material, data on protest events, and newspaper accounts. After this introduction, we briefly review the literature on the normalization of protests and the ways in which social movements can contribute to shape politics. We then offer an overview of the political context in which the student movement emerged. The next two sections analyze the effects of the student movement to present days. To conclude, we discuss the student movement's main contribution to politics in Chile so far and future prospects.

NORMALIZING PROTEST AND SHAPING POLITICS

Early work on social movements focused on demonstrators' psychological features and commonly argued that mass mobilization was the result of rapid changing societies and the institutional difficulties to channel emerging sources of discontent (Smelser 1962). An implicit idea of this scholarship was that protest constituted something exceptional and was not part of "normal politics." In other words, taking part in a social movement was an unconventional form of political participation. In this view, the conventional way was to partake in elections. Another assumption was that it socioeconomically disadvantaged people that protested, as this was the only mechanism available to them to push for change.

From the protest wave of the 1960s onwards, these conceptions gradually changed (Meyer and Tarrow 1998, 4). For one, more protests events took place across the world. Secondly, it became increasingly evident that not only poor people participated in demonstrations. For example, the feminist, environmental, and peace movements, were largely composed of middle-class sectors with access to education (della Porta and Diani 1999, 36). Thus, not only were there more diverse constituencies protesting, but there was also a broader range of claims at stake. Thirdly, the institutionalization and professionalization of social movements also contributed to the wider acceptance of protest as a conventional feature of politics.

Meyer and Tarrow (1998) famously referred to societies that witnessed these three processes as social movement societies. They argued that in industrialized democracies such as the United States and Western European countries, demonstrations and other repertoires of action have become a recurrent and acceptable part of the political game. Citizen engagement expressed in marches and other repertoires of action complements electoral participation and allows to signal citizen preferences and concerns on specific policy issues. The normalization of protest involves new opportunities for advancing social movement agendas, as it means more presence both on the streets and in the institutional terrain. Rather than the negative view on protest activities that dominated early scholarship on social movements, Meyer and Tarrow (1998), among many others, therefore consider social mobilization to be a sign of a more participatory democracy.

Accepting protests as part of the functioning of politics in modern societies also involved focusing on their consequences. Social movements can have a wide array of effects. There is a substantial amount of literature on the cultural, organizational, and biographical effects that movements can produce. The focus in this chapter is on their political outcomes. These can be expressed in the impact on the public agenda, a specific policy outcome, or even institutional change. There are abundant historical examples of social movements that have been crucial in their countries' political histories. The civil rights movement in the United States, for example, defined a new benchmark in terms of rights for the historically marginalized African American community (Andrews 1997). Social movements also played a crucial role mobilizing against authoritarian regimes in various parts of the globe (Hipsher 1998; Nikolayenko 2017).

Social movements commonly tend to phase out. As the concept of protest cycle denotes, over time, there is a decline of collective action. It is therefore somewhat surprising that they can have such impact on politics. However, many times social movements institutionalize and continue to affect politics with other means. According to Meyer and Tarrow (1998, 21), social movements have institutionalized when their organizations become professionalized and their interactions with institutional actors more routinized. Additionally, institutionalization of a social movement is expressed by its inclusion in mainstream institutions. Finally, social movements can be regarded as undergoing a process of institutionalization when they "alter their claims and tactics to ones that can be pursued without disrupting the normal practice of politics" (Meyer and Tarrow 1998, 21).

In a similar vein, research drawing on the political process model has shown that the impact that social movements can have after phasing out ultimately depends on the political allies that they are able to have. As a bourgeoning literature has explored, what has been referred to as institutional activists play a central role in advancing social movement claims in the political arena. For example, research on Brazil's universal health movement has shown that activists who joined the state apparatus when democracy was reinstated, launched an equity-enhancing health reform "from within" (Weyland 1995; Gibson 2019). Similarly, in the case of the feminist movement in the United States, institutional activists were successful in implementing reforms to tackle workplace pregnancy discrimination (McCammon and Brockman 2018). In addition, by forming political parties and disputing political power, social movements can bring their claims to the decision-making arena. Recent literature on movement-parties—political parties that emerge from social mobilization—has shown both the potential and limitations of new parties such as Podemos in Spain and Syriza in Greece (della Porta et al. 2017). In sum, then, even when protest activity phases out, social movements can impact politics in numerous ways.

DEMOBILIZATION AND POLITICAL DISENCHANTMENT IN DEMOCRATIC CHILE

One of the great paradoxes of Chile's recent history is that civil society was more active during the dictatorship than in the first decade of democratic rule (Oxhorn 2011, 104). While various social movements mobilized against the military regime in the 1970s and especially in the 1980s, once democracy was reinstated in 1990, demobilization became the new norm. There are manifold reasons for this. For many social movement leaders who had mobilized alongside the opposition parties, backing the *Concertación*, the newly formed center-left coalition that gained power, was as a way of supporting democracy (Burton 2009, 60). This also meant that social movements were more likely to withhold demands and to avoid pursuing strategies that could threaten democratic stability (Hipsher 1998, 155). As Hipsher (1998, 157) argues, social movement activists often envisioned a long-term rationality in demobilizing. The fact that there often was an overlap between social movements and political leaders also contributed to the demobilization of social movements. Finally, the *Concertación* governments—four in total—did not prioritize building institutions that could strengthen civil society in general and foster political participation in particular (Delamaza 2014). As a result, until the 2000s, social movements played a marginal role in shaping politics in Chile.

Protests spearheaded by high school students in 2006 placed the issue of education on the public agenda (Donoso 2013). But it was not until the rise of the student movement in 2011, in which both high school and university students participated, that broader socio-political processes that had been in the making since the reinstatement of democratic rule in 1990 crystalized.

First, students articulated extant discontent with the neoliberal education reforms developed since the mid-1970s. As the movement repeated once and again in the numerous rallies organized during 2011, Chile's education system segments students according to their families' financial capacity. This education system was introduced during the military regime (1973–1989), but was then left relatively unchanged by the *Concertación*. Inspired by the thought of Milton Friedman, the military junta and its civilian allies, introduced strong incentives for the expansion of the private education market. At the primary and high school levels, a subsidiary-based system was implemented to facilitate the creation of private schools (Borzutsky 2002, 176). New state-subsidized private schools proliferated and created a three-tier system that also included private schools without state funding and public schools. This had as an effect that the poorest students were left at public schools, and that the learning outcomes tended to be segmented according to type of school (Valenzuela et al. 2014). On the positive side, it significantly increased student enrolment at both primary and secondary school levels (Cox 2005, 23). In higher education, state funding to public universities was cut and many private universities were founded without much regulation (Zurita 2015). The *Concertación* was unable to modify the structural bases of the education model introduced by the military. While reforms were introduced to increase the quality of education, socioeconomic segmentation remained a key feature of the country's education system.

Second, the student movement exposed the growing discontent with political institutions in Chile. During its four consecutive governments, the *Concertación* had to govern within the frame of the constitution introduced by the Pinochet junta in 1980. This limited the space for policy reform. Yet, from the perspective of the students that mobilized, a significant part of the center-left coalition was convinced of the benefits of the neoliberal model (Grau 2013; Lira 2014; González 2014). The signs of citizen discontent with both the functioning of democracy and the contents of the political game were numerous. The percentage of Chileans that consider that democracy works badly or very badly increased from 20 percent in 2012 to 40 percent in 2016. Those who stated that democracy is preferable to any other political regime declined from 64 percent in the same time period. At the same time, the percentage that claimed that the Parliament drafts and approves bad and very bad laws increased from 49 percent in 2010 to 78 percent in 2016. Clearly, political parties in general, not only on the center-left, were having problem representing the will of the citizenry. Not surprisingly, as shown in Figure 3.1, identification with political parties declined steadily during the four consecutive *Concertación* governments and continued to do so after 2011.

PROTEST WAVES AND POLICY EFFECTS

To understand the rise of the student movement in 2011 and its political impact, it is necessary to depict the organizational development that made it possible. Indeed, its emergence was not spontaneous, but rather the result of years of organizational development linked to previous protest waves. In the first years after the reinstatement of democracy, the student movement declined. After having played a key role in the fight against the military regime, during the 1990s it struggled to construct an agenda that resonated with public opinion. University student federations organized in the *Confederación de Estudiantes de Chile* (CONFECH), which served as an umbrella organization. Yet, it was only toward the end of the 1990s when the CONFECH gained force again, mobilizing for greater internal

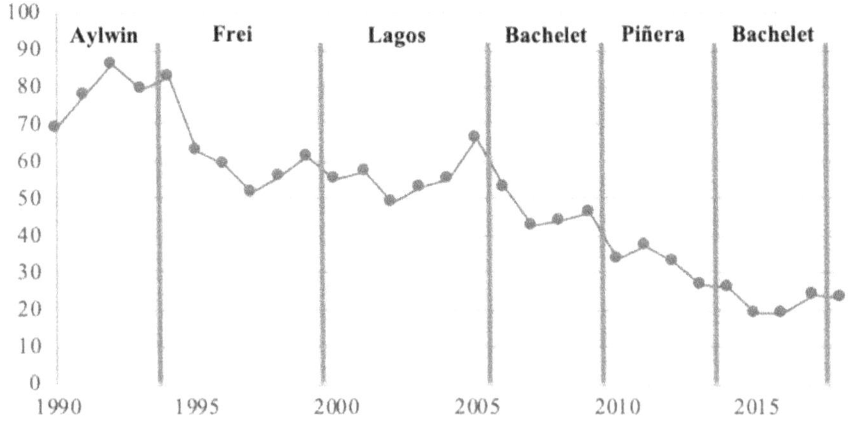

Figure 3.1 Percentage of Party Identification (1990–2018). *Source*: Adapted from surveys by the Centro de Estudios Públicos (CEP), 1990-2015.

democratization in the universities and more funding for public education, among other issues.

A similar development took place at the level of high school student organizations. Here, the traditional umbrella organization, the *Federación de Estudiantes Secundarios* (FESES), was replaced by new organizations such as the *Asamblea Coordinadora de Estudiantes Secundarios* (ACES) and later, the *Coordinadora Nacional Estudiantes Secundarios* (CONES). These organizations constructed an agenda based on demands related to the improvement of infrastructure, cheaper school transport pass, and university entry exam, among others. Both at the university and high school levels, new left-leaning political organizations such as the *Surda*, critical of the communists and its top-down approach to politics, gained influence (Figueroa 2019).

In 2001, the first massive student protests were led by high school students grouped in the ACES. This mobilization became known as the *Mochilazo*[1] and was motivated by the Ministry of Education's delay in delivering the school pass to the students. The students were outraged not only by the postponement, but also about the fact that the passes were issued by an organization that brought together private transport companies. This meant that when the conflict erupted, the educational authorities referred to the issue as a matter between private entities. After weeks of protests, which gathered thousands on the streets of Santiago, the Ministry of Education finally gave into the student demands. The authorities agreed to both overseeing the administration of the school pass and reducing its cost. Despite the specific nature of the subject in question, the students who led the *Mochilazo* valued their triumph. As one former student leader argued, this conquest meant that the state recognized its responsibility in securing that students were able to attend school (Reyes 2011).

Importantly, high school students could build on this victory in future mobilization efforts. Five years later, in 2006, student protests gained force again. President Michelle Bachelet had just started her first government (she won the presidential elections in 2013 again) when a school in southern Chile was destroyed by pouring rain, revealing the precarity of school infrastructure. This triggered demonstrations in both the capital and in regional cities. Clashes with the police motivated a second repertoire of action that was less dangerous for the students. School takeovers served to legitimize the student movement in the eyes of public opinion as the students centered on discussing the faults of the education model in the schools and raise awareness.

In contrast to the 2001 *Mochilazo*, the 2006 movement—known as the *Pingüino* (penguin) Movement due to the students' black-and-white school uniforms—lasted for many weeks and was nationwide. The government response was also more encompassing. This time, the president and not only the education authorities addressed the students. Michelle Bachelet, who just a few months earlier had won the presidential elections on a campaign with a strong emphasis on citizen participation, instituted an advisory commission to discuss the education model (Donoso 2013). Student representatives were invited to participate. Yet, the movement was neither satisfied with the way in which deliberation was undertaken in the commission, nor its results. The commission was composed of education experts and actors across the political divide. While recognizing the deficiencies of the education system, many of the commission members favored solutions that were different from those proposed by the students. Hence, the report that the commission submitted to the government did not entail an overhaul of the education model as the movement leaders had hoped.

Nevertheless, the resulting reforms implemented in the years that followed the rise of the *Pingüinos* aimed at introducing more equality, accountability, and regulation in an education system that previously was highly unregulated (Bellei et al. 2010). The Bill on Preferential Subsidy, approved in 2008, involved more resources to schools with the most vulnerable students. The Constitutional Law of Education (LOCE) was replaced and mechanisms that give the state a more central role in the provision of education were introduced. This included aspects such as the physical and institutional conditions and administration of the education system, and norms related to the teachers. While emphasizing the quality of education, the new General Law of Education (LGE) consolidated the mixed provision of education, that is, the existence of public, state-subsidized, and private schools. Finally, the Agency on the Quality of Education, approved in 2011, aimed at guaranteeing higher standards in both the learning processes and learning achievements.

From the perspective of the *Penguin* movement, the government response to its demands was experienced as treason. Indeed, as social movement scholars have argued (della Porta and Diani 1999, 162), there are ambivalent implications for the development of a social movement when establishing a working relation with the authorities. On the one hand, the public recognition that this involves and the access to decision-making arenas illustrate their impact. On the other hand, discontent provoked by what many times is viewed as a negotiation with the authorities can limit a movement's mobilization capacity, thus weakening it in the long run. The lesson left by the 2006 mobilization and the participation in the presidential advisory commission was to distrust the traditional parties grouped in the *Concertación*. As a result, disconnection between student organizations and the center-left parties deepened.

Between 2006 and 2011, discontent with the education system grew. In 2010, the center-right won the elections for the first time since 1990 and Sebastián Piñera, one of the country's richest persons, became president. This contributed to the rise of the 2011 student movement in several ways.

It unified high school and university students and also the various left-wing political organizations that commonly disputed the presidencies of the university federations in a common struggle. Secondly, the Piñera government's lack of responsiveness to the massive mobilizations that carried on during most of 2011 increased extant discontent. It also led to the student movement widening its petition to also include a new political constitution that allowed to change the power balance in Parliament (changing the quorums to pass reform, for example) and eliminate the subsidiary role of the state.

One of the starting points of the 2011 student protest wave was at the Universidad Central, one of the country's many private universities. Following the announcement that a significant share of the university was being sold to a private company, students feared that the university's pluralistic, secular, and independent spirit would be lost in the hands of the new owners. Their demonstrations were supported by students from other universities. The situation at the Universidad Central was regarded an expression of the faults of a privatized education model. Another example of this was the student loan scheme with the state as a guarantor that President Lagos, from the Socialist Party, had created in 2006 to enable students from lower socioeconomic background to access higher education. In 2011, more than 310,000 students had enrolled in this scheme and were highly indebted, creating a fertile soil of disgruntlement (Rivera et al. 2018, 94).

When Sebastian Piñera won the elections in 2010, many of the student organizations grouped in the CONFECH prepared for a year of mobilization. An exhaustive discussion of the education system and elaboration of a diagnosis had been undertaken in 2009 when students organized a congress with different actors of the education sector. The fact that the country was hit by an earthquake in 2010 forced the postponement of any mobilization effort to 2011. Just as the delay of the school pass in 2001 and the poor infrastructure revealed by the rain season in 2006, the situation at the Universidad Central constituted a triggering event. From May 2011 onward, both university and high school students mobilized across the country, occupied their buildings and called for public, free education. The first response of the government came after several weeks of protests. The measures that were proposed, mainly more access to university loans, were widely considered insufficient. At the beginning of August, police repression after a rally in Santiago motivated a call for a *cacerolazo*—the hitting of pots as a way of protesting. This was highly symbolic as this repertoire of action was recurrent during the dictatorship and had not been employed since then.

Importantly, both in 2006 and 2011, the student movement garnered support from public opinion. According to survey data from 2006, 87 percent of Chileans supported the student demands (OECD and World Bank 2009, 29). Surveys from 2011, in turn, showed that almost 80 percent of Chileans agreed with the student demands (Adimark 2011). Furthermore, as illustrated in Figure 3.2, education as a policy priory increased among Chileans both in 2006 and 2011. Protest had proven effective as a mechanism to influence the public debate.

While the response of the Piñera government to the student movement was reduced, in the next electoral campaign the center-left led by Michelle Bachelet promised to address the issues raised by the students. After winning the elections in 2014, her administration passed a set of reforms that aimed at tackling inequality in the education system. First, to address the issue of socioeconomic segregation in schools, the School Inclusion Law was passed in 2016 which prohibited schools that receive state funding from selecting their students. In 2017, the Bachelet government passed the Law on Public Education, which initiated a process of centralization of the school system redirecting some of the responsibilities of the administration of the schools from the municipalities to the Ministry of Education. Finally, a reform to higher education introduced free-of-charge tuition for the poorest students and a set of measures to strengthen public universities. Corruption scandals involving family members of President Bachelet considerably weakened her government. In part, this explains why more education reforms were not undertaken during the rest of her presidency.

THE NORMALIZATION OF PROTESTS IN CHILE

Throughout the protest waves in 2001, 2006, and 2011 previously described, Chile's student movement grew in importance and presence in the public

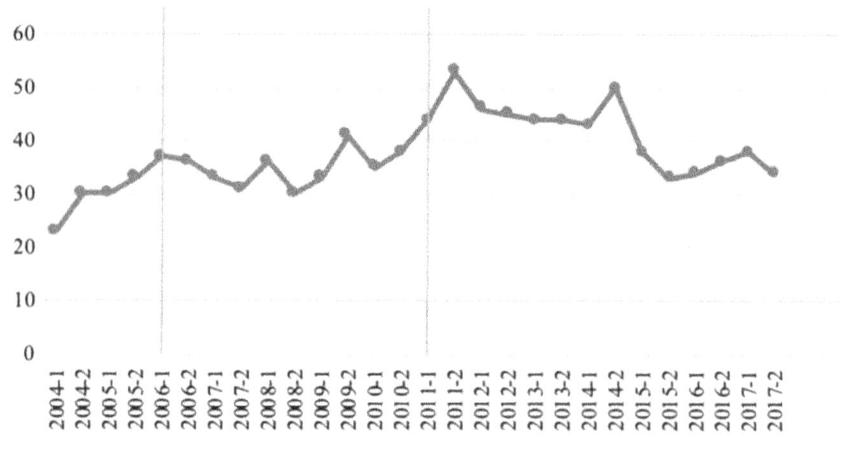

Figure 3.2 People Mentioning Education as a Priority (%). *Source*: Adapted from surveys by the Centro de Estudios Públicos (CEP), 2004-2017.

debate. Chileans became gradually accustomed to the rise of student protests, especially in the beginning of the academic year. In early April every year, both high school and university students started mobilizing to push for deeper reforms to the education system. At the high school level, both the ACES and the CONES consolidated their position as the main representative student bodies. With yearly elected spokesperson, these organizations became known by the public and political authorities and were the principal convening actors when manifestations were staged. At the university level, the CONFECH professionalized their work, especially in relation to their communication practices. This meant having a person in charge of the relationship with media outlets, and also a more extensive use of social media (Roa 2014; Martínez 2014). After 2011, the CONFECH also broadened the scope of universities that it represented. While historically the umbrella organization only comprised public universities that belong to the Council of Presidents of Chilean Universities (CRUCH), from that year onwards also some private universities created in the 1980s were included. Hence, more students were represented by the CONFECH, the organization widened its constituency and gained force.

After years marked by demobilization, protests in general and led by students specifically became a recurrent feature of the country's political life. The routinization of collective action, defined as the process through which both challengers and authorities can "adhere to a common script, recognizing familiar patters as well as potentially dangerous deviations" (Meyer and Tarrow 1998, 21) has thus also been part of the contribution of Chile's student movement.

Importantly, recurrent student protests were accompanied by mobilization processes led by other actors. Figure 3.3 illustrates the evolution of protest events related to indigenous, environmental, labor, and regional demands, which also rose from the 2000s onwards. It shows that between the years 2000 and 2012, contentious acts spearheaded by students constituted an important proportion of the total number of protest events, but it was far from being the only actor in mobilizing.[2] Moreover, not only did the number of protest events increase gradually from the 2000s onwards, but also the number of people participating in them (Somma and Medel 2017, 36).

Furthermore, extant data shows that the acceptance of protests is also high. Between 2006 and 2014, the percentage of Chileans that approved of protest varied between 50 and 60 percent (Latinobarometer, various years).[3] Among young people between 18 and 24 years, the percentage is even higher: 70 percent. This greater acceptance among youth is similar in other parts of the globe. One reason might be that young people tend to participate more in non-conventional forms of politics , such as demonstrations, and are therefore more familiar with the experience and value as being better than do older cohorts. It

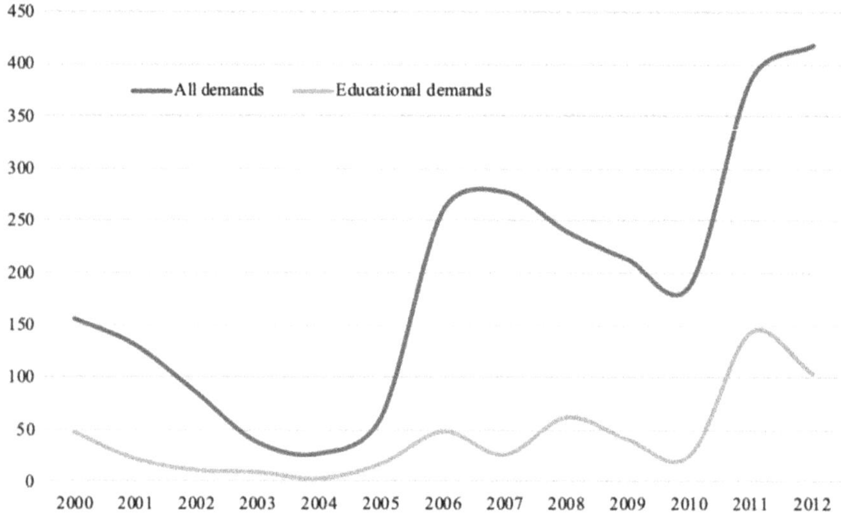

Figure 3.3 Number of Protest Events in Chile (2000–2012) by Type of Demand. *Source*: Protest events in Chile database 2000-2012, Fondecyt Iniciación 11121147, PI Nicolás M. Somma.

is important to note, however, that more people approve of protest than participate in them. While the array of social movements has widened significantly in the last decade in Chile, the percentage of people that participate in them varies between 10 and 20 percent. Again, this is not different from global trends.

As previously noted, the support of public opinion support to the student movement, in particular, was very high during the peak of mobilizations in 2011. From that year onwards, CEP surveys show that confidence in the student movement gradually declined, although with some increase again in 2017 (CEP surveys, various years). Not surprisingly, the student movement is especially valued among young people. Finally, the COES-ELSOC (2019) survey shows that between the years 2016 and 2018, 92 percent of Chileans declared that they value at least one social movement that was active in the last three years. The survey lists the following social movements and asks whether the person surveyed supports any of them: student, labor, environmental, indigenous, sexual diversity, anti-abortion, anti-delinquency, feminist, and pensions. The student movement is the alternative that receives the most support, although it declined slightly in 2018. This is followed by the labor movement and the anti-delinquency movement, both of which also have lower levels of support in 2018. In sum, the student movements and other social movements have a considerable level of support in public opinion, yet this support is not set in stone and tends to be linked to particular protest waves in which the issues raised by the movements gain public attention.

OPENING UP THE POLITICAL SPACE

The institutionalization and professionalization of the social movement organizations that comprise the student movement, the routinization of their yearly protests, and their acceptance by public opinion have transformed the student movement into a conventional feature of Chilean politics. As described above, this presence translated into significant policy debates and reforms in the realm of education. This way, the case of the student movement in Chile confirms that the strength of social movements is central to impact decision-making processes (e.g., Gamson 1975; Minkoff 1997; Soule and King 2006). Yet, both the 2006 and 2011 protest waves left an important lesson about the limitations of social mobilization alone as a way of putting pressure on the political system. Their development and political response confirmed what existing scholarship has argued, namely, that social movements are most likely to influence the policy-making process at the early stage of policy formulation (Soule and King 2006, 1877).

The year 2011, in particular, showed that despite having reached an unprecedented level of mass protests, the political response to the student movement was reduced. This motivated putting forward new demands that went beyond the field of education more forcefully. A new constitution that replaced the one enacted during the military regime therefore became part of the rallying cries of the 2011 protest wave.

A growing awareness of the insufficiency of street protests alone also inspired the decision of a group of student leaders to compete in parliamentary elections. In the 2013 general elections, two former student leaders, Giorgio Jackson and Gabriel Boric, were elected. At first, the fact that President Bachelet proposed an education reform as a key pillar of her government program complicated these leaders' capacity to construct a convincing discourse that could contribute to keep up the spirit of the student mobilization. However, as President Bachelet started to lose support as a result of a series of corruption scandals and the details of the proposed education reforms became clearer, Jackson and Boric, in particular, became important critics of the pace and the content of the promised changes to the education model.

This critical role and distancing from the Bachelet government motivated not only the creation of Jackson's and Boric's own political parties, but also the institution of a political coalition that gathered different political organizations with strong presence in the student movement and other social movements such as the one against the pension system. In early 2017, the Frente Amplio was formally created. It was motivated by the shared goal to build an alliance that went beyond an electoral pact. In the words of one former student leader, "the bet that we have been building since 2006 [year of the *Pingüino* movement] is to turn politics around in Chile" (Hidalgo 2019). During the previous two decades, the different left-leanings political groupings that had attempted to gain political representation that went beyond the *Concertación* and the center-right coalition had failed to keep unified. Therefore, the Frente Amplio made a substantial effort to construct a shared political platform that could serve as a guide in the long term. After Frente Amplio' launch in 2017, it launched an ambitious schedule of local reunions to construct a government program from the bottom-up and a website with different participatory mechanisms.

In 2015, the Bachelet administration passed a law to change the binomial electoral system, which was bequeathed by the military regime and whose design included incentives to the construction of broad alliances, to the detriment of smaller, independent political forces. The binomial electoral system was thus part of the reason why Chilean politics, until then, was dominated by two big blocs. In practice, it also allowed for significant overrepresentation of rural areas and of the right (Angell and Reig 2006, 496). The change to a proportional inclusive electoral system during the Bachelet government aimed at introducing more representativeness, especially for different regions, and less barriers for independent candidates. Among other things, the new system increased the number of deputies from 120 to 155 in order to improve representativeness. The introduction of the new electoral system favored the Frente Amplio. In the 2017 elections, the new political coalition established itself as a third political force with significant levels of parliamentary representation by electing twenty deputies and one senator. The coalition's presidential candidate obtained 20 percent of the vote, almost making it to the second round. With this result, the Frente Amplio radically changed the political game in Chile, opening it up for new political forces more critical of the country's development model and political system.

CONCLUSION

This chapter depicted the evolution of the student movement in Chile and its role in making protest a normal feature of politics and opening up the political space. After many years of depoliticization and demobilization of civil society, successive protest waves led by students allowed institutionalizing the main student organizations and routinizing the way in which their demands are put forward. Yet, they also involved a gradual but marked distancing between student organizations and the traditional political parties on the center-left. The policy changes left after the main student protest waves were deficient from the perspective of the students. Awareness of the formal and informal institutional constraints to enact reforms that could reverse the neoliberal logic of the education model also convinced many student leaders that mobilization alone was insufficient to reach their goals. In 2017, this motivated the creation of a third political force in Chile: the Frente Amplio. This move can, in part, be considered a way of institutionalizing the demands of the student movement. Scholarship on social movements has long debated about the effect of the institutionalization of protest. In the case of the student movement and its presence in the Frente Amplio, it clearly has involved difficulties. Trying to have "one foot on the streets, and one foot in Parliament," as many Frente Amplio leaders expressed they would when gaining their parliamentary seats has been a challenge in the context of Chileans' profound distrust in political institutions. At the same time, it has been an opportunity to push for a political agenda from Parliament.

Since the last elections—in which Sebastián Piñera and his center-right coalition came into power for the second time—Chile's political and institutional difficulties have deepened. In October 2019, protests initiated by high school students escalated and caused an unprecedented political crisis. In turn, this forced a parliamentary agreement to change the country's current constitution as a way of ending the crisis. In the near future, therefore, Chileans will be discussing the rights and duties that they wish to establish as the basis for the future construction of citizenship. Many of the issues pushed for by the student movement in the last two decades is part of this agenda.

NOTES

1. The word stems from "mochila," which means backpack.
2. This protest event database was constructed by one of the authors of this chapter by coding newspaper reports published by the *Observatorio Social de América Latina* (OSAL).
3. This means that on a scale between 1 and 10 where 10 is more acceptance, people chose 7 or more.

REFERENCES

Adimark. 2011. 'Quoted in Cooperativa.cl 'Adimark: Apoyo al movimiento estudiantil subió al 79 por ciento.' (https://www.cooperativa.cl/noticias/pais/politica/encuestas/adimark-apoyo-al-movimiento-estudiantil-subio-al-79-por-ciento/2011-10-05/121430.html)

Andrews, Kenneth. 1997. 'The impacts of social movements on the political process: The Civil Rights Movement and black electoral politics in Mississippi.' *American Sociological Review* 62(5): 800–819.

Angell, Alan, and Cristóbal Reig. 2006. 'Change or continuity? The Chilean elections of 2005/2006.' *Bulletin of Latin American Research* 25(4): 481–502.
Bellei, Cristián, Daniel Contreras, and Juan Pablo Valenzuela. 2010. 'Viejos dilemas y nuevas propuestas en la política educacional chilena.' In *Ecos de la revolución pingüina*, edited by Cristián Bellei, Daniel Contreras, and Juan Pablo Valenzuela, 11–30. Santiago, Chile: Pehuén Editores.
Borzutsky, Silvia. 2002. *Vital connections: Politics, social security, and inequality in Chile*. South Bend: University of Notre Dame Press.
Burton, Guy, and Jonathan Sands. 2009. *Social democracy in Latin America: Policymakers and education reform in Brazil and Chile*. London: London School of Economics and Political Science.
Centro de Estudios de Conflicto y Cohesión Social (COES)-Estudio Longitudinal Social de Chile (ELSOC). 2019. 'Radiografía del cambio social. Análisis de Resultados Longitudinales Estudio Longitudinal Social de Chile.' (https://coes.cl/encuesta-panel/)
Centro de Estudios Públicos. 2016. 'Estudio Nacional de Opinión Pública N° 78.' (https://www.cepchile.cl/cep/encuestas-cep/encuestas-2009-2018/estudio-nacional-de-opinion-publica-noviembre-diciembre-2016)
Centro de Estudios Públicos. 2017. 'Estudio Nacional de Opinión Pública N° 81.' (https://www.cepchile.cl/cep/encuestas-cep/encuestas-2009-2018/estudio-nacional-de-opinion-publica-septiembre-octubre-2017)
Centro de Estudios Públicos. 2018. 'Estudio Nacional de Opinión Pública N° 82.' (https://www.cepchile.cl/cep/encuestas-cep/encuestas-2009-2018/estudio-nacional-de-opinion-publica-octubre-noviembre-2018)
Cox, Cristian. 2005. 'Las políticas educacionales de Chile en las últimas dos décadas del siglo XX.' In *Políticas educacionales en el cambio de siglo. La reforma del sistema escolar de Chile*, edited by Cristián Cox, 19–113. Santiago, Chile: Editorial Universitaria.
Delamaza, Gonzalo. 2014. *Enhancing democracy: Public policies and citizen participation in Chile*. New York and Oxford: Berghahn Books.
della Porta, Donatella, and Mario Diani. 1999. *Social movements. An introduction*. Oxford: Blackwell Publishing.
Donoso, Sofia. 2013. 'Dynamics of change in Chile: Explaining the emergence of the 2006 Pingüino movement.' *Journal of Latin American Studies* 45(1): 1–29.
Figueroa, Francisco. Interview by Sofia Donoso. 9 December 2019. Santiago, Chile.
Gamson, William. 1975. *The strategy of social protest*. Belmont, CA: Wadsworth Press.
Gibson, Christopher. 2019. *Movement-driven development: The politics of health and democracy in Brazil*. Stanford: Stanford University Press.
González, Gabriel. Interview by Sofia Donoso. 26 June 2014. Santiago, Chile.
Grau, Nicolás. Interview by Sofia Donoso. 27 April 2013. Brighton, United Kingdom.
Hidalgo, Andrés. 2019. Interview by Sofia Donoso. 28 September 2019. Santiago, Chile.
Hipsher Patricia. 1998. 'Democratic transitions as protest cycles: Social movement dynamics in democratizing Latin America.' In *The social movement society:*

Contentious politics for a new century, edited by David S. Meyer and Sidney Tarrow, 153–172. Lanham, MD: Rowman & Littlefield Publishers.

Lira, Julio. Interview by Sofia Donoso. 6 February 2014. Santiago, Chile.

Martínez, Javiera. 2014. Interview by Sofia Donoso. 23 January 2014. Santiago, Chile.

Mayer, David, and Sidney Tarrow. 1998. *The social movement society*. Lanham, MD: Rowman & Littlefield Publishers.

McCammon, Holly, and Amanda Brockman. 2018. 'Feminist institutional activists: Venue shifting, strategic adaptation, and winning the pregnancy discrimination act.' *Sociological Forum* 34(1).

Minkoff, Debra. 1997. 'The sequencing of social movements.' *American Sociological Review* 62(5): 779–799.

Nikolayenko, Olena. 2017. *Youth movements and elections in Eastern Europe*. Cambridge: Cambridge University Press.

OECD and World Bank. 2009. *Revisión de políticas nacionales de educación: La educación superior en Chile*. Paris: Organisation for Economic Cooperation and Development Publishing.

Oxhorn, Philip. 2011. *Sustaining civil society: Economic change, democracy, and the social construction of citizenship in Latin America*. University Park: Pennsylvania State University Press.

Reyes, Julio. Interview by Sofia Donoso. 15 November 2011. Santiago, Chile.

Rivera, René, Víctor Climent, Almendra Espinoza, and Pablo Rivera. 2018. 'Financiamiento de la Educación Superior en Chile a través del Crédito con Aval del Estado (CAE). Una oportunidad para la inclusión o el aumento de la brecha social.' In *Políticas Públicas para la Equidad Social*, edited by Pablo Rivera-Vargas, Judith Muñoz-Saavedra, Rommy Morales-Olivares, and Stefanie Butendieck-Hijerra, 93–102. Santiago, Chile: Colección Políticas Públicas—Universidad de Santiago de Chile.

Roa, Giovanna. 2014. Interview by Sofia Donoso. 29 January 2014. Santiago, Chile.

Smelser, Neil. 1962. *Theory of collective behavior*. New York: The Free Press.

Somma, Nicolás, and Rodrigo Medel. 2017. 'Shifting relationships between social movements and institutional politics.' In *Social Movements in Chile*, edited by Marisa vön Bulow and Sofia Donoso, 29–61. New York, NY: Palgrave Macmillan.

Soule, Sarah, and Brayden King. 2006. 'The stages of the policy process and the Equal Rights Amendment, 1972–1982.' *American Journal of Sociology* 111(6): 871–909.

Valenzuela, Juan Pablo, Cristian Bellei, and Danae de los Ríos. 2014. 'Socioeconomic school segregation in a market-oriented educational system. The case of Chile.' *Journal of Education Policy* 29(2): 217–241.

Weyland, Kurt.1995. 'Social movements and the state: The politics of health reform in Brazil.' *World Development* 23(10): 1699–1712.

Zurira, Andrés. 2015. 'El sistema universitario en el Chile contemporáneo.' *Educação em Revista* 31(2): 329–343.

Chapter 4

Defending Education

Student Resistance to the Educational National Assessment System in Chile

Pablo Santibáñez-Rodríguez

INTRODUCTION

Educational systems around the world are currently sites of deep conflict about the role and value of education. As in so many other countries, recent government-imposed educational reforms in Chile have triggered serious debate and conflict about the purpose of education. High school students in Chile are key players in the development and implementation of national education policies. From the "Save our School" movement in the United States[1] to the Occupations of Public Secondary Schools in Rio de Janeiro (Brazil), high school students have become central actors in the development of education policies. Schools have become spaces for conflicting imaginaries about the role education should, and does, play in the development of a society. Considering these tensions, in this chapter, I document the contemporary student movement in Chile, as well as the government's reaction to the students' activism.

Chilean high school student activism has been a dimension of Chilean history for almost a century (Salazar and Pinto 2010). From protests against the increased transport costs and occupations to restore a democratic government, high school students have played a major role in Chilean social movements. In this chapter, I explore answers to two main questions: How have student protests challenged education policy in Chile? How have Chilean educational policy-makers and other key actors involved in the field responded to these student movements? To answer these questions, I refer to a range of secondary sources including newspapers and audio recording from students from 2015 to 2018, as well as interviews with students. I synthesize my findings through a storytelling model, which identifies the subjects, objects, receivers, helpers, and opponents in both student and government narratives. The proposed analysis is based on the "actantial approach" developed by the Lithuanian literary scientist Algirdas Greimas (1987). Greimas used this approach to explore the forms in which different social groups represent their views about different topics in "actants"[2] that are constant in each social group narrative as follows (Duvall 1982):

- Subject: The main character of the narrative represented in the texts.
- Object: The aim that is pursued by the subject.
- Receiver: Characters or contexts that are benefited for the achievement of the object.
- Helpers: Characters or contexts that increase the opportunities of achieving the object.
- Opponents or traitors: Characters or contexts that harm the opportunities of achieving the object.

This chapter focuses on the implications of student activism for educational policy in Chile. The students' actions reveal the emergence of an alternative imaginary that posits that national assessments thwart the possibility of reaching the full potential of a quality education for all students. Through the protests, the relationship between students and government officials presented a changing inflection. The first government elected in 2014 included students' demands in the policies that regulated the application of national assessments. However, the second government elected in 2017 developed policies that sought to erase students' involvement in policy. With this background in mind, I highlight the existence of a disputed terrain on educational communities in Chile. While the student protests in Chile articulated new educational imaginaries, the impact of the national/conservative agendas that are embedded in the Chilean state, have a longer and deeper connection to neoliberal policy trajectories than countries like the United States and the United Kingdom (Hooge et al. 2012).

CONTEXT: THE NATIONAL ASSESSMENT FOR QUALITY EDUCATION IN CHILE

Government officials operate on the assumption that Chile's Educational National Assessment System (*Sistema de Medicioİn de Calidad de la Educacioİn—SIMCE)* measures the quality of students' learning in reference to the National Curriculum (Meckes and Carrasco 2010). During the last three decades, the "Educational Quality Agency," the agency responsible for evaluation and guidance of the Chilean educational system, has used the test results to define the quality of public and private schools. In addition, various private educational agencies measured the evolution of the national assessment system (SIMCE) scores to identify "excellent schools,"[3] which secure a strong comparative advantage in the school's competition for student's enrolment (Falabella 2014). Nevertheless, studies reveal that the interpretation of scores influence market competition and deepen the gap between private and public schools (Mizala and Torche 2012). The SIMCE scores were interpreted without including variables such as the social and cultural backgrounds of students (that largely explain in Chile as elsewhere how well student perform academically). As a consequence, many families and students moved from traditional public schools to private or charter schools assuming it would enable their children to get higher scores. The public schooling system was converted into a space mostly for those who were not able to pay for their schooling.

The national assessment system (SIMCE) is part of a thirty-year-old global educational practice called "New Accountabilities." This global enterprise promotes standardized testing and audit cultures in the school (Lingard 2010, 2011; Lingard et al. 2015). It is a new perspective with affinities to the more general neoliberal political project, started during the 1980s. Globalization also encouraged the implementations of new accountability principles such as management, the use of market criteria, and performance metrics (Spina 2017). Critical scholars have highlighted the problems with this "governance by numbers," including how it curtails the development of alternative curriculum and pedagogies (Biesta 2008; Lingard 2011; Hooge et al. 2012; Jankowski and Provezis 2012; Lingard et al. 2015; Ashadi and Rice 2016; Rushek 2016).

Nevertheless, certain scholars are calling for research that analyzes the role that educational communities play in contesting and rejecting this auditing and accountability practice. Some scholars document how teachers, parents, and students work to play a role in renegotiating and stopping the spread of neoliberal policies and new accountabilities practices in particular (Keddie et al. 2011; Gowlett 2013; Lipman 2013). This chapter takes up these perspectives to argue that current trends in global student activism demonstrate how the "new accountabilities" movement has become a key catalyst for boosting a student movement that works as a counterweight against extreme economic approaches on educational policy.

THE SCHOOL OCCUPATIONS AGAINST NATIONAL ASSESSMENTS

The student mobilizations that started in 2006 ushered in a new period of contestation over the direction of educational policy in Chile. The movement of high school students, called the "Penguin Revolution," and the university student-led "Chilean Winter" directly challenged the Chilean educational system (Bellei and Cabalin 2013; Peñafiel and Doran 2018; Pickard and Bessant 2017). Since 2011, these student movements have criticized the way the national assessment system (SIMCE) has redefined the concept of "quality" in education. For example, students began to denounce the techniques developed by schools to increase SIMCE test results, which led to a drastically narrower curriculum in schools. High school students in Concepcion staged their first actions in support of an alternative policy during the test day of 2015. The students' occupations of schools made it impossible for official assessment teams to get into the schools to administer the tests.

My first question focuses on understanding the aims of the actions developed by Chilean student activists. In their occupation of their schools, students were intent on contrasting their ethical and moral understanding of education with the national assessment system (SIMCE) and the neoliberal values embedded in the test. A student representative during the 2016 mobilizations explains it this way:

> We oppose the application of SIMCE because the test segregates and buries public education . . . This standardized test does not measure all the knowledge of students across the different schools in Chile. (President of Enrique Molina Garmendia high school students' union 2016)

For students protesting their opposition to the SIMCE, the test is a tool to defend public education against the marked inequality and social segregation that already exists in the educational system. Student activists point to different scholars to argue that the existing degree of socioeconomic segregation has close ties with the "new accountabilities" paradigm. According to Elacqua (2012), Chilean students from high-income families tend to study in better and more expensive schools, while students from low-income families are more likely to study in free public schools that are typically characterized with lower educational quality. Rather than attack this pattern of social inequality in education, the use of the SIMCE test tends to further embed inequality in the schooling system. In addition, the students question the forms in which tests are used to define the funding for schools as well as the real benefits for students. Students argue that the test constricts the development of different kinds of knowledge in schools:

> They point out that it is a tool to evaluate and improve the quality of schools. (. . .), but what is the quality of education? (. . .) In all the formal documents associated with SIMCE, there is no definition of "Quality of education" (. . .) the government's conceptualization of quality of education is reductionist. For

> them [the government], the quality of education corresponds only to the score obtained in SIMCE. (Gajardo, Interview, 2018)

In this way, these students are questioning the fundamental purpose of education. For them, the national assessment system (SIMCE) works as a test that reduces the purposes of education. Students argue that the nature of education is being analyzed from a simplistic approach. The students are aware that different epistemic values are privileged in the test, which then trickle down into curriculum and instruction. In other words, students are aware that their curriculum is narrowing due to reforms in accountability.

In the next sections I provide my analysis using a storytelling model. I identify and discuss the subjects, objects, receivers, helpers, and opponents in both student and government narratives. In order to address that aim, I analyze the narratives that emerge from students' representatives, students, political figures from all spectrums as well as official interviews from government authorities.

The Students as the Performers of an Alternative Imaginary

In their narrative of their activism, the protesting students represent themselves as actors who are part of a longer story of historical activism in their schools. During the occupations, students pointed to a long trajectory of actions, invoking a historical memory of student activism. For example, one of the representatives who was interviewed in 2019 process said:

> We are all the children of the working class and we will never be ashamed of that. And because we are children of public education, we will continue to be the face of public education, and we are not going to take the test, we won't be bootlicking this market-oriented test . . . This high school is the only one in Chile not taking the test for the 4th consecutive year! (Students spokesperson 2018)

Student activists stress their social class when talking about themselves. While they are highly critical of a segregated educational system, they understand that social exclusion is part of their identity as children of the working class. At the same time, they assume an identity as champions of the public system: they are prepared to defend the system against what they understand to be market-oriented tests. These students represent themselves as a subject linked to the working class and workers' struggles which is a crucial element in their repudiation of the national assessment system (SIMCE). They believe that the way the government uses this test harms them directly. They reject the competitive ethos fostered by SIMCE because they understand that this exacerbates the already entrenched inequalities between private and public schools.

Mobilization and Face-to-Face Organization against a Market-Oriented SIMCE

From 2014 to 2018, student organizations in Chile mobilized against SIMCE. Their mobilization transformed the schools into places where students decided to be part of the policy-making process. The main ways of sharing the information during their mobilization ranged from direct interaction in assemblies to sharing information on online social networks like WhatsApp, Facebook groups, and the student union Instagram page. However, students indicated that they preferred to avoid the use of social networks when organizing and developing actions because of the possibility that their networks or mobiles were monitored by police or other state agencies. For instance, one student explained:

> We organize [events] at school . . . We use the Students' Union's Facebook and Instagram pages to diffuse [our mission], but we have our discussions about organizing face-to-face. (Gajardo, Interview, 2018)

While students recognized the relevance of social media networks, students preferred face-to-face relationships due to the monitoring and surveillance of authorities through fake social network profiles. For students, these tactics provided information to authorities about the planned actions of student protesters before they took place. As a result, the students needed to change or expand their repertoire of forms of activism:

> We all live in the same precarious school. History tell us that our problems have only been solved through mobilization (. . .) we have to march , we have to occupy schools, we have to strike, we have to improve. (Students spokesperson 2 2018)

The students used their previous experiences with activism as well as other social movements to inform their activist organization. When they speak about possible actions to develop, they indicate that there is the need to consider actions that were previously effective in pressuring different authorities. For example, during their assemblies, students expressed that direct mobilization was necessary to achieve their goals. To decide which actions to take, they first discussed previous actions that were successful in creating change, then they voted collectively among these options.

Students' Actions Challenged by Government and School Administrators

In developing their strategies, student protesters also identify other groups or people who might either help or hinder the achievement of their objectives. My research indicates that students are not always able to identify groups that can support them during an occupation. Rather, students can more easily identify likely obstacles or opponents. For students, government and school employees are typically the main obstacles to the realization of their activism. As one student during the assembly held in 2018 put it:

> Now we are criminalized and judged. The teachers and administrators deliberately come to our student group's meetings. But we are not afraid, this vote will reach everyone, it will be transversal, it will be universal, everyone will be informed. (Students spokesperson 3 2018)

Students are well able to identify certain members of the school or the education bureaucracy who are likely to want to criminalize them and aim to suppress, or at least weaken, the student organization. They have highlighted the lack of privacy during the process, and the interest of some teachers, schools' principal, and school counselor in blocking the student movement. For students:

> There are teachers that agree this is something worth fighting for, and the rest do not care. The school principal wants to eliminate all types of organizations, because they believe that this causes low enrollment. They removed the keys from the Student Center room and called all the parents [of student] representatives to inform them that they would expel three students. The school principal told to our parents that our actions were supported by political parties. (. . .). For having access to the Student Center room they threatened the student president last year, because he was at the door. (Gajardo, Interview, 2018)

Students' Organization for Defending the Public School System

An important element of the framework developed by students has been to identify the beneficiaries of the student movement's activism. Those involved in the student movement are the chief beneficiaries of their actions, but during the protests the students indicated that their actions are intended to represent all students in the public school system who are harmed by the application of the national assessment (SIMCE), specifically students from socioeconomically vulnerable and rural schools:

> How is it possible that SIMCE defines the schools funding? How is it possible that the schools that perform better on national assessments receive more funding? The schools that need more help because are underperforming will receive less funding! The lower results in SIMCE is because they [the schools] are in rural areas without basic material conditions! (President of Enrique Molina Garmendia high school students' union 2016)

The students indicate that the allocation of resources based on the national assessment test (SIMCE) scores do not actually improve the quality of education. They highlight the inability of the system to distribute resources intelligently because schools with low test results do not perceive additional resources. This factor was a catalyst in the mobilization: to present the case that the low test results of those schools are best explained by social or economic poverty. Students were also concerned about effects of SIMCE on their future as undergraduate collegiate students. They argue that as university students, they will need knowledge and skills that are not being developed in their high school because the schools are preoccupied with preparing them to do well on the SIMCE tests: "The academic demands of Universities are not going to be reduced to what the SIMCE evaluates us on. Our schools haven't prepared us for [the rigors] of college" (Student spokesperson 2018).

THE RELATIONSHIP BETWEEN POLICY AND SCHOOL OCCUPATIONS DURING THE "CULTURAL CLASH" ON EDUCATION

The school occupations have been a crucial topic on the debate about education in Chile. From 2014 to 2018, a coalition of political parties led by Michele Bachellet ruled the country.[4] One of the reasons cited for their victory was their claim that they would include many of the student movements' demands on their agenda (Bellei et al. 2018). As a result, the Educational Quality Agency (*Agencia para Calidad de la Enseñanza)* proposed a reduction on the number of tests in schools and future changes to transform the national assessment test (SIMCE) from a census-based test toward a sample-based test. In other words, the proposal was to shift from testing every student to testing a sample of students that would represent the population. In addition, the organization allowed the comparison of SIMCE results only between schools with similar socioeconomic backgrounds. This aimed to reduce the prejudice at work in highlighting certain schools framed as a binary of "good" or "bad" schools.

However, the acknowledgment and incorporation of student demands into educational policy changed after the December 2017 elections. A new coalition government led by Sebastián Pinera, based on four center-right and right political parties, represented those opposed to the reforms carried out by the Bachellet government. During 2018, the new government made changes to educational policy introduced from 2014 to 2018. The first change was the "Safe Classroom." Based on specific instances of violence in some schools in Santiago, the government promoted a law that would accelerate the expulsion of students that participated in violent acts of activism. However, the political motivations behind this policy went beyond that.

One of the key elements of this analysis is to understand the objectives of the government's actions. During 2018, the Pinera government outlined its intentions for the new law. Pinera said:

> We hope that this bill will allow us to restore tranquility, peace and the right climate so that children and young people have all the tools to fully develop their potential. (Dinamo 2018)

Government officials indicated that the central objective of their actions was to achieve educational "quality." By this they meant the cultivation of a community that possesses "physical and psychological integrity." For President Pinera, the aim is to reestablish something that had been lost. For the government, this bill seeks to reestablish an appropriate climate in the classroom to promote competencies to be learned in the schools. This feeling of restoring a lost peace, of recovering a favorable climate for learning, created a context for questioning the student occupations. This theme was taken up and developed by certain media outlets with conservative agendas. During the debates about the bill, a television report explored the "political indoctrination" carried out by some teachers in public schools. Specifically, the report linked students at one high school to a guerrilla group that had used political violence against Pinochet's dictatorship. The report was immediately denounced as "fake news." Students explained that the evidence shown by the TV report corresponded to a pedagogical activity where the students portrayed the role of women in one of the guerrilla groups. The government came out in support of the TV report, claiming this was evidence of the need to approve the "Secure Classroom" bill:

> Channel 13 released a report last night of situations that were previously known and published which relate to the actions of groups within the "Liceo 1." These actions (. . .) have generated, as we have seen, various disturbances, disorders, [and] exercise a sort of cooptation of the High Schools. (El Mostrador 2018)

The government's reaction to this TV report suggests that the objective of the "Secure Classroom" bill was duplicitous. On the one hand, it seemed to promise improving the quality of education in a flawed system. On the other hand, it had a political objective, namely the promotion of a specific discourse about the school as a politicized space used for promoting "deviant" and sometimes radical views of society. During the debates about the bill, political and conversational panels discussed the legitimacy of high schools for the organization of student movements.

The Government as the Defender of the Educational Communities

The government represented itself as the main character that defends the educational community from the menace of violence. For example, President Pinera commented:

> Our Government is, and will always be, with the professors who want to teach; with the students who want to learn (. . .). We will always fight, and with great force, those who want to destroy our school community. (Pinera 2018)

The analysis shows the government, as a subject, that communicates to its people that it wants to secure the welfare and peace of the educational community. In this way, the government claims to be the "champion" of quality education. The government's mission is to preserve the peace and alleviate the violence that has taken over the community. In addition, from government statements, it is possible to discern a subject that works as an adversary for the government's narrative: the student organizations. The government expressed that student organizations dismantle the peace and safety of educational institutions. As President Pinera put it:

> I want to call all my compatriots and especially the parliamentarians, this is not to be confused, one thing is the students, the school community, and a very different thing are criminals disguised as students who do not tremble before anything or anyone. (Pinera 2018)

The government also encouraged TV reports to broadcast images of teachers "politicizing students." For example, the previously detailed case of a television news reporter showing a picture of student "guerilla" activists. The photograph was taken out of context, as the students were acting in a play for their history and social sciences class. The government used those TV reports to promote a negative image of the student organizations that participate in those events. For government officials:

> There are precedents in relation to the Liceo 1 that realize that there are names of adults who are part, as a kind of coordinators, trainers, and inspirers, of a group

> of girls and who may have or have had relationships with previous movements [that were] violent as the Manuel Rodríguez Patriotic Front. (Chadwick 2018)

According to the government, these student organizations are influenced by adults. The student subject is represented from a passive point of view, unable to develop let alone act out their own ideas. The government officials removed student agency and autonomy from their resistance, and represent them as puppets co-opted by manipulative adults who instruct them and lead them into violence. This reflects the way in which the law created a context for highlighting images developed before the "Secure Classroom" bill. President Pinera clearly characterized student organizations as groups that thwarted the capacity of the state to run a quality education system. Throughout the debate, the government consistently emphasized the radicalism of the students who participate in these events:

> I call for us to promptly process the Safe Classroom bill that will give us tools to remove criminals from the schools who often disguise their uniforms to generate anarchy. (Pinera 2018)

This is how the discourse changed during the process of development and discussion of the law. In describing specific actions carried out by students, the government indicated that their adversaries were now "criminals" disguised in school uniforms trying to promote anarchy.

The Educational Agenda for Expelling Violence Outside the School

The "Secure Classroom" bill had a clear action focus on "security":

> To have a quality education we need to have security. Without security in the classroom we will not have quality in any room in the country. (Pinera 2018)

Interviews with government officials help explain the real aim of the bill, which goes beyond the explicit messages found in the bill. These interviews shed light on the values and political interests that guided the construction, defense, and implementation of the "Secure Classroom" bill. In summary, the objectives of the bill provided for immediate expulsion and cancellation of registration in the case of students using, possessing, and storing weapons as well as any acts of physical aggression that result in injuries to any member of the educational community (Ministerio de Educación 2018).

While the actions targeted by this new law are indefensible, there remains the need to analyze the interviews in which the government revealed their deeper interests: to demonize student organizations. Therefore, analysis of additional actions that can reveal implicit elements and objectives must be included. In developing the law, a series of additional actions emerged with the aim of establishing in the public opinion the necessity of this law. Faced with these actions, oppositional spokespeople denounced the concealed intentions driving the development of this law:

> We all know that these acts of extreme violence, which we all repudiate, are basically concentrated in four schools of Santiago so many doubts have arisen. (Soy Temuco 2018)

I now highlight the intentions and motivations that lay behind the "Secure Classroom" bill. The law was a response by the government to the violence that occurred in four schools of the capital region, a tiny fraction of the 16,000 schools in Chile not affected by this kind of violence.

In the Chilean educational system, there are different ways principals and school administrators can expel and punish students for committing violent acts. For example, administrators can call a specific council that can accelerate the expulsion process. Furthermore, the few schools affected by the extreme violence indicates the problem was specific to local communities rather than across the entire educational system. However, government officials revealed their focus much wider than the specific cases of violence.

In addition, the government's communication strategy included disseminating misinformation, as evidenced in the television report that connected student activism with former guerrilla groups. The government's intention was to do more than simply combat extreme violence. All the strategies developed by the government show that the real intention was to weaken one of the fundamental bases of the student movements: the use of schools as a space to develop alternative visions of education.

Opposition to the Bill as Accomplices of Violence

The government identified "the congress' opposition" as the main hindrance to achieving quality education. The government utilized the rhetoric surrounding a violent act in which a group of students attacked a police officer during a national protest to stress this idea. This incident was questioned by all political factions and student leaders, and used by the government to increase public support for the bill.

Various student groups opposed the "Secure Classroom" law and indicated that it sought to generate a negative image of students. They argued that the law would be used to punish their organizations. The government responded by arguing that those who opposed the bill were siding with "the criminals." In this way, the government represented the opposition to the bill as a new obstacle to their bid to achieve and develop "quality education." The following interview excerpt with one government official shows how the claim that those who opposing the bill were represented as supporting students who carried out violent actions. A pro-government senator puts it this way:

> I say it straight: the president of the commission of Education, Yasna Provoste, has become an accomplice of the violence to stop a priority project. (Moreira 2018)

Those who questioned the effectiveness of this bill were represented by the government as accomplices to violence. Here there is a movement away from a political debate and a motion toward a good and bad binary, between "violence" and "peace" and low and high quality education. This set of dichotomies have been used to represent educational reformers as accomplices of violence. After eight years of relevant changes on educational policy, this bill represents the first step taken by defenders of the status quo to fight back.

The "Secure Classroom Bill" as the Last Resource for Defending Teachers and Families

The government defined some groups as beneficiaries of the "Secure Classroom" bill. My research indicates that the people most likely to benefit from legislation are represented as the victims of student violence. The first of these groups are the teachers. During September 2018, the Minister of Education Marcela Cubillos said:

> A teacher is obliged to live, during the 30 days that delay the process, in the same classroom with the student who sprayed it with benzene or assaulted him, which is completely inhuman and unworthy. (Dinamo 2018)

From the government's perspective, the teacher is the main victim of student violence, and needs protection. Government officials stress the idea that the bill will accelerate the expulsion of students from their schools, and therefore reduce the negative impact on teachers who are required to continue teaching students who may have earlier assaulted them. During the public discussion of the law, the government persisted with this line arguing that the time to "be political" was over: As one government official explained:

> Let's forget about making speeches for promoting political figures. Can we talk about the people's real issues? In our country there are teachers who are afraid

> of going to work. In our country, the school's neighbors see how their streets are vandalized by these criminals. (Pinera 2018)

According to government officials, politicians had not understood the fear experienced by teachers. Additionally, there was the problem of the damage to schools and public infrastructure caused by the student protests. Therefore, to pass the legislation, a key narrative the government used during the development of the law relied on an interesting political construction setting "society" against "politics." While "society" seeks protection from the law, the "politics" defend the criminals, that is, the students who harm society.

CONCLUSION: STUDENT ACTIVISM AND EDUCATIONAL POLICY

In this chapter, I introduce three ideas that reflect the role and current state of Chilean student activism. I stress the need to enter into dialogue with more global aspects of student activism, as well as with the study of educational policy both locally and globally.

The students' occupation of schools during the application of the national standardized test (SIMCE) in Chile involved a process of policy subjectivation. This means that students empowered themselves as relevant actors in the policy-making process. During their protests, students decided to question the form in which educational quality was administered by the government. The school occupations developed by students were processes that openly contested the imaginary of education developed by the market-oriented Chilean schooling system. The students challenged the rationality that linked a certain model of "evidence-based policy" with neoliberalism. Students argued that the complex nature of education, claiming to show "what works" was not working (Biesta 2007). In the occupations staged against SIMCE, the students contested the value of measuring educational quality using standardized tests. The student occupations revealed the capacity of students to outline the principled basis of their opposition to educational policy. The students' resistance argued that SIMCE presented an overly simplified perspective on education, and that the process of measuring educational quality was actually more complex.

The students' diagnoses reflected the segregation of knowledge generated by SIMCE. In other words, student organizations moved from being silent in the policy-making process toward proposing policy initiatives. Students' activism was situated between historical precedents and a new repertoire of political activism. To achieve their objectives, students developed a politics that connected historical student activism with new uses of technologies and social networks. While there is plenty of evidence that young activists used new technologies, there is little evidence about the role that memory and history played in their repertoire of actions. I identified a melting pot of actions that mixed historical learning as well as the use of contemporary tools. Like their predecessors in the 2006 and 2011 student campaigns, students used different tools for disseminating their messages as well publicizing their main actions (Santibáñez-Rodríguez and Ganter-Solís 2016). However, they were also making sense of the ways that authorities and police also used the same techniques to suppress their movement. For example, by developing fake profiles on Facebook and Instagram, schools and authorities collected and used information on online social media accounts as evidence to justify imposing sanctions on student protesters. This tactic by authorities pushed students to reconsider online use and return to face-to-face relationships. Therefore, new technologies and social networks are not always considered as a space for action, rather can also be considered as a space for the dissemination of information.

There is a major cultural clash in education as schools became sites of contestation between conservative and progressive subjectivities. Consequently, the schools and educational communities constituted the space for the tension between different imaginaries on education.

While this chapter has focused on Chile, schools across the globe represent a key battleground for the clash between deep-rooted global neoliberal subjectivities and alternative imaginaries. Across the globe (as other chapters in this volume show), student movements have organized actions to contest the dominant imaginaries in the field of education. Student activism has revitalized a debate about what education is *and* ought to be. In other words, organized student movements have been able to reignite a debate that had been forgotten in different places around the world. From an apparent consensus about education during the 1990s, student activism questioned the neoliberal imaginaries that underpinned educational policy as well as racism, sexism, and patriarchy. However, their impact on the development and implementation of educational policies needs to be subjected to critical reflection. The reactions from the current Chilean government, and the support obtained by the "Secure Classroom" bill is an example of this. While seven years ago the support from public opinion to student-led social movements in education was clear and strong (80 percent), nowadays these numbers have changed dramatically.

Rather than romanticize the impact of student activism on educational policy, we need to understand and critically explore the forms in which this non-neoliberal imaginary highlighted by students has been embraced by public opinion and educational communities. Furthermore, the relevance of the school as a battleground for the clash between different subjectivities needs to be carefully explored under the current global context, as different countries experience the emergence of right-wing populisms that promote authoritarianism, conservatism, and nationalism. Consequently, the conceptualization and development of educational policy needs to be revisited in a context where students as well as conservative groups assume the right and the capacity to speak. On the one hand, there is an urgency surrounding the need to recognize the intellectual equality of students. There is also a case for thinking further about the role that educational communities have played in introducing policies embedded in deeply rooted neoliberal subjectivities.

The last fifteen years of student mobilizations in Chile reveal that student activism has become the main source for sustaining an alternative model of educational policy. Deep-rooted neoliberal imaginaries imposed on the community sustain a market-oriented/conservative view of education. Some of the initial policies motivated by students are vigorously rejected by parents, principals, and teachers. The counter action coming from the government toward students who are engaged in the occupations enjoys strong support from the public. This also highlights the value in continuously paying attention to the different practices students use in becoming hegemonic/subaltern political actors.

NOTES

1. Save Our Schools is a grassroots volunteer organization which seeks to increase the role of the community when considering educational reforms in areas such as leadership, funding, and accountability.
2. An "actant" can be defined as a role that is typically present in storytelling. Following the *Oxford Dictionary of Literary Terms* (1996), the concept can be understood as "six basic categories of fictional role common to all stories."
3. While the concept of excellence in education is highly controversial, different foundations have sold to schools external assessments that conducted to seals of excellence. An example of this was the "School management quality seal" by Chile Foundation that was given to more than 2,500 schools around Chile which included between their most important indicators the improvement of SIMCE scores.
4. Former president and minister of defense from 2006 to 2010. During her first election, Michele Bachellet was known for her conflicts with student organizations. However, during her second presidential campaign, she ran as the candidate who was "in touch with the people."

REFERENCES

Ashadi, Ashadi, and Suzanne Rice. 2016. 'High Stakes Testing and Teacher Access to Professional Opportunities: Lessons from Indonesia.' *Journal of Education Policy* 31, no. 6: 727–741. https://doi.org/10.1080/02680939.2016.1193901.

Bellei, Cristián, and Cristian Cabalin. 2013. 'Chilean Student Movements: Sustained Struggle to Transform a Market-Oriented Educational System.' *Current Issues in Comparative Education* 15, no. 2: 108–123.

Bellei, Cristián, Cristian Cabalin, and Víctor Orellana. 2018. 'The Student Movements to Transform the Chilean Market-Oriented Education System.' In *Civil Society Organizations in Latin American Education*, 63–84. Routledge.

Biesta, Gert. 2007. 'Why 'What Works' Won't Work: Evidence-Based Practice and the Democratic Deficit in Educational Research.' *Educational Theory* 57, no. 1: 1–22.

Biesta, Gert. 2008. 'Good Education in an Age of Measurement: On the Need to Reconnect with the Question of Purpose in Education.' *Educational Assessment, Evaluation and Accountability* 21, no. 1: 33–46. https://doi.org/10.1007/s11092-008-9064-9.

Chadwick, Hernán. 2018. 'Alumas Y Apoderados Desmienten Reportaje De Canal 13 Sobre 'Adoctrinamiento' En El Liceo 1.' *El Mostrador*, 22 October 2018.

Dínamo, El. 1982. 'Pinera Presenta 'Aula Segura': El Proyecto Que Busca Sancionar a Los Estudiantes Que Participen En Actos De Violencia.' *El Dínamo*, 20 September 2018, 2.

Duvall, John. 1982. 'Using Greimas' Narrative Semiotics: Signification in Faulkner's The Old People.' *College Literature* 9, no. 3: 192–206.

El Mostrador. 2018. 'Alumas Y Apoderados Desmienten Reportaje De Canal 13 Sobre 'Adoctrinamiento' En El Liceo 1.' *El Mostrador*, 22 October 2018.

Elacqua, Gregory. 2012. 'The Impact of School Choice and Public Policy on Segregation: Evidence from Chile.' *International Journal of Educational Development* 32, no. 3: 444–453. https://doi.org/10.1016/j.ijedudev.2011.08.003.

Falabella, Alejandra. 2014. '¿Qué Cambiar Del Simce?'. *Cuaderno de Educación* 61, no. 1: 1–14.

Gajardo, Lautaro. 2018. *El Día Del Simce (the Day of Simce)*. Concepción.

Gowlett, Christina. 2013. 'Queer(Y)Ing New Schooling Accountabilities Through My School: Using Butlerian Tools to Think Differently About Policy Performativity.' *Educational Philosophy and Theory* 47, no. 2: 159–172. https://doi.org/10.1080/00131857.2013.793926.

Greimas, Algirdas Julien. 1987. *Semantica Estructural.* Madrid: GREDOS.

Hooge, Edith, Tracey Burns, and Harald Wilkoszewski. 2012. *Looking Beyond the Numbers: Stakeholders and Multiple School Accountability.* OECD.

Jankowski, Natasha, and Staci Provezis. 2012. 'Neoliberal Ideologies, Governmentality and the Academy: An Examination of Accountability Through Assessment and Transparency.' *Educational Philosophy and Theory* 46, no. 5: 475–487. https://doi.org/10.1080/00131857.2012.721736.

Keddie, Amanda, Martin Mills, and Donna Pendergast. 2011. 'Fabricating an Identity in Neo-Liberal Times: Performing Schooling as 'Number One'.' *Oxford Review of Education* 37, no. 1: 75–92. https://doi.org/10.1080/03054985.2010.538528.

Lingard, Bob. 2010. 'Policy Borrowing, Policy Learning: Testing Times in Australian Schooling.' *Critical Studies in Education* 51, no. 2: 129–147.

Lingard, Bob. 2011. 'Policy as Numbers: Ac/Counting for Educational Research.' *The Australian Educational Researcher* 38, no. 4: 355–382. https://doi.org/10.1007/s13384-011-0041-9.

Lingard, Bob, Wayne Martino, Goli Rezai-Rashti, and Sam Sellar. 2015. *Globalizing Educational Accountabilities*. Routledge.

Lipman, Pauline. 2013. *The New Political Economy of Urban Education: Neoliberalism, Race, and the Right to the City*. Taylor & Francis.

Meckes, Lorena, and Rafael Carrasco. 2010. 'Two Decades of Simce: An Overview of the National Assessment System in Chile.' *Assessment in Education: Principles, Policy & Practice* 17, no. 2: 233–248. https://doi.org/10.1080/09695941003696214.

Ministerio de Educación. 2018. *Gobierno Envía Al Congreso Proyecto De Ley 'Aula Segura'*. Santiago: Ministerio de Educación.

Mizala, Alejandra, and Florencia Torche. 2012. 'Bringing the Schools Back In: The Stratification of Educational Achievement in the Chilean Voucher System.' *International Journal of Educational Development* 32, no. 1: 132–144. https://doi.org/10.1016/j.ijedudev.2010.09.004.

Moreira, Ivan. 2018. 'Moreira Y Dichos De Provoste Por Aula Segura: 'Se Ha Convertido En Cómplice De La Violencia'.' By Tomás Molina. *Emol*.

Peñafiel, Ricardo, and Marie-Christine Doran. 2018. 'New Modes of Youth Political Action and Democracy in the Americas: From the Chilean Spring to the Maple Spring in Quebec.' In *Young People Re-Generating Politics in Times of Crises*, pp. 349–373. Palgrave Macmillan.

Pickard, Sarah, and Judith Bessant, eds. 2017. *Young People Re-Generating Politics in Times of Crises*. London: Palgrave Macmillan.

Pinera, Sebastián. 2018a. 'Aula Segura: Pinera Condena Ataque a Carabinero Y Llama a Parlamentarios a Apoyar Proyecto.' *Tele13*, 12 October 2018.

Pinera, Sebastián. 2018b. *Presidente Pinera Promulga Ley Aula Segura: 'Nuestro Gobierno Está, Y Va a Estar Siempre, Con Los Profesores Que Quieren Enseñar; Con Los Alumnos Que Quieren Aprender'*. Santiago: Ministerio Secretaría General de Gobierno.

Rushek, Kelli A. 2016. 'The Global Education Reform Movement and Its Effect on the Local African American Community.' *Diaspora, Indigenous, and Minority Education* 1–9. https://doi.org/10.1080/15595692.2016.1219848.

Salazar, Gabriel, and Julio Pinto. 2010. *Historia Contemporánea De Chile V: Niñez Y Juventud*. Santiago de Chile: LOM Ediciones.

Santibanez Rodriguez, Pablo, and Rodrigo Ganter Solis. 2016. 'Representaciones sociales de lo político: Convergencias y divergencias del relato generacional en el gran Concepción.' *Ultima década* 24(44): 39–70.

Spina, Nerida. 2017. 'Governing by Numbers: Local effects on Students' Experiences of Writing.' *English in Education* 51, no. 1: 14–26. https://doi.org/10.1111/eie.12109.

Temuco, Soy. 2018. 'Senador Quintana Criticó El Proyecto De Ley 'Aula Segura' Presentado Por El Gobienro.' *Soy Chile*, 20 October 2018.

Chapter 5

Student Political Action and Activism in Contemporary Nigeria

Joseph Egwurube

INTRODUCTION

The way higher education students in developing countries and particularly in Africa are organized, both institutionally and nationally, how their interests are aggregated, articulated, and intermediated by state authorities and how they have tried to determine the content and direction of public choices has been the focus of academic research (Emmerson 1968; Hanna 1975; Lulat 1981, 234–266; Boahen 1994; Federici et al. 2000; Boren 2001; Konings 2005, 161–188; Zelig 2007; Nyamnjoh et al. 2012; Luescher et al. 2016; Luescher and Klemencic 2017, 113–128). There is good reason to explore the landscape of university student organizations in Nigeria and the different expressions of students' claims. This is because there is a vision of Nigerian university students as the country's future elite, as clients of educational policies, and as a constituency (Luescher et al. 2016, 18). An examination of their attitudes, their demands, their forms of action and the major on-campus and off-campus questions they address, is clearly useful if we are to get any insight into the challenges of governance and public crisis management in Nigeria.

Scholars and politicians conventionally undervalue the importance of university students' claim-making in their bid to understand how national priorities are set and resources mobilized for two main reasons. The first involves qualifying such claim-making as unstructured, transient, and unruly or brutal, due to the sometimes short-lived or even violent forms they have taken as expressions that almost invariably breach the peace. The second reason is the "monolithic, militaristic and often dictatorial political systems" characteristic of African states (Omar and Mihyu 1991, 4). In other words, in countries where the opportunities for political and social pluralism are restrained and where those in power are wont to monopolize rather than share decision-making, any inclination to enable "active minorities" like university students (Hanna 1975, 71–101) to determine the direction and pace of public resource allocation is deemed to be a fruitless exercise.

I do not agree with these assertions because I do not think that university students in Nigeria are powerless and disempowered. First, even if protests, not all of which are violent, have become the dominant form of expression by students, such protests clearly qualify as an informal form of expressing student interest on particular policies (Luescher et al. 2016, 9–10). Secondly, the university in Nigeria is a "protected space" (Brennan et al. 2004, 33), usually located several kilometers away from adjoining cities, where campus-based political activism, under the protection of academic freedom, has enabled university academics and students in particular to legitimately question regimes, regime leaders, regime behavior, national sociopolitical, and economic programs, and express their opinions on the policy options proposed by public authorities. Thirdly and most importantly, public decision-making in Nigeria is not as monolithic and as closed as some profess (Odo et al. 2014).

The assignment of priorities and definition of solutions is open to influence from civil society which is very well organized in Nigeria (Harbeson et al. 1994). According to one researcher, Nigeria has "a vibrant civil society in which the mass media, trade and professional unions, students' associations, human and civil rights groups have been able to act as an effective counterweight against the state" (Mgba 2015, 183). I believe that the increasing use of the social media by university students (Eke et al. 2014; Amadi and Ewa 2018), facilitates intercampus and interuniversity communication, which in turn increases the mobilizational capacity of students. The increasing pressure for government transparency and accountability, coupled with the failure of the state to address the social and economic needs of millions of Nigerians, gives credibility to dissenting voices. Public policy-making is thus open to debates, and to inputs from university students, even if these are frequently dissenting and oppositional.

This study will examine the level of activism by university students. Student activism is intrinsically political because the claims these students activists make are expressions their intention to maximize their access, and the access of other groups of Nigerians' access, to resources. In this way they hope to directly influence public resource allocation. Two sources of data will be used. First, I use secondary literature to examine how students are organized and how they have tried to articulate their demands on the process of the public agenda setting. I also use the results of fieldwork done in 2018 in a Nigerian university, where I administered a questionnaire to over 400 students on several issues linked to student activism.

This chapter is divided into five sections. First, I define and clarify the concept of student power and activism in Nigeria. I determine the sources of student power and the resources students exploit to legitimize their claim-making before presenting the paradigm I use. Then, I turn to student unionism and student governance and assess the autonomy with which students can organize themselves without dictates from tutelary authorities. The third section focuses on concrete cases where student activism has been expressed, with a view to assessing the outcome of such activism in terms of policy output. The fourth section provides an analysis of student attitudes and expectations, using the results of my fieldwork. In the conclusion, I suggest that students will continue to count on public agenda setting even though they are formally excluded from public decision-making structures.

STUDENT POWER IN NIGERIA

My conception of student power goes beyond the "revolutionary student movement" perspective first advanced by Cockburn and Blackburn (1967). I do not think that Nigerian university students are powerful because they are in a position "to create an extra-parliamentary opposition which aims to reconquer power from below" or that they wish to control the organization and content of the education they receive (Cockburn and Blackburn 1969, 7). Rather, my use of the concept of student power is largely informed by Klemencic's "agentic" model (Klemencic 2015, 11–30). Klemencic introduces the theory of student agency to the examination of student engagement. For Klemencic, student agency encompasses two notions, that of agentic possibility, which is related to power, and that of agentic orientation, which is linked to the will to act. For the author, "students are likely to be 'agentic', that is they seek to exert some influence on their educational trajectories, their future lives and their immediate and larger social surroundings" (Klemencic 2015, 11).

The following definition of "student power" by another writer, clearly uses this agentic idea. I agree with Lapidus when he says:

> I believe power means that students have the ability to identify problems and solve them in the face of bureaucratic and institutional obstacles. It means setting a goal and having the communication network, the strategy, the physical numbers, and the commitment to achieve it. It means the fair representation of students in political and social issues. It means building the society we want rather than simply accepting the society into which we were born. (Lapidus 2013)

Several sources of student power can be identified in Nigeria. These sources can be treated as enabling resources for the exercise of this kind of power. The first is the willingness by students to act, even when the odds are against them. The fight against British colonial masters by students under the umbrella of the West African Students Union led by Ladipo Solanke, a Nigerian, is a case in point (Boahen 1994). The willingness of the National Union of Nigerian Students (NUNS) to question some of the choices made by successive military regimes, ultimately ending up in the banning of the Union under the Obasanjo military government in 1978, is another case in point. A second student body, the National Association of Nigerian Students (NANS), was established in 1980 to replace the banned union.

Another resource is the belief by students in the legitimacy and the efficacy of their actions. This relates to the "self-efficacy" element or the belief in the "capacity to exercise control over events" (Klemencic 2015, 14). The different instruments—individual, proxy, and collective—that can be used to translate this belief into action have been explored by Bandura (Bandura 2001).

Then, there is the numerical strength of university students in Nigeria. The country today has more than 1.9 million students enrolled in more than eighty public universities, half of which are federal government managed (N.U.C 2017). These universities are geographically spread over the entire national territory and their sheer number, along with their geographical spread, provides students with a potent and forceful bargaining argument to make claims on federal authorities.

Additionally, the public tends to have a soft spot for students who are considered to be the leaders of tomorrow and as the conscience of the nation (Adelabu and Akinsolu 2009). Therefore, because students believe they are the spokespeople for the silent and toiling majority, a definition that is never openly contested, students see their fight as legitimate when they get caught up in a tug-of-war or a head-on collision with public authorities in making their claims.

Another source and resource is the clearly demonstrated failure of successive federal governments to satisfy the promise of political independence and guarantee the average Nigerian, usually described as "the common man," a desirable standard of living. The delayed take-off of economic development and the increasing number of Nigerians who live under the "poverty line" are accompanied by an ever-increasing incidence of corruption including embezzlement of government funds, which lends credibility to questions students raise about the principles, directions, and outcomes of public governance.

A sixth and final source of the agentic power of students in Nigeria is, of course, their knowledge or their access to knowledge. Compared to other kinds of Nigerian citizens, university students believe they are more aware of the ills of society and claim to have the necessary intellectual wherewithal to judge if government policies will combat these ills.

The university campus in Nigeria is thus an academic, social, and political space. It is an academic space because it is designed to stimulate creative and rigorous thinking by students. The space also gives them the necessary intellectual tools to conduct research on, and better understand, their society. The university campus is equally a social space because it facilitates interaction between peers, between genders, between adults and the young, and between people from different stations in life, regions, and backgrounds. This creates a confrontation of worldviews, which nurtures and refines the student community both individually and collectively. Interaction with others improves knowledge of those others, and encourages students to question their preuniversity-held beliefs, stereotypes, values, and opinions. The campus is also the epitome of a political space. Political opinions are fearlessly exchanged because the university community is founded on academic freedom, including freedom of thought. The Nigerian university is a political space because it is an area where different social and political paradigms are variously shared, debated, or contested. Questions are regularly asked by students about the quality of government policies, whether these are student-centered or society-centered. University autonomy offers students better opportunities for political engagement, for the refinement of their political values, for their political socialization and for getting a better understanding of the political world (Adelabu and Akinosolu 2009, 51). The campus offers a convenient environment for appraising, judging, and contesting national regimes, regime actors, and regime behavior without censorship.

It is possible to conceptualize the capacity of Nigerian students to exert influence over their educational trajectories, to improve their conditions of living and to change the way society functions in relation to four sets of variables. The first concerns the level of knowledge university students have about the evidence and political values that inform the design of public policy and its intended objectives. Students also vary in their levels of understanding about why, for example, a government has adopted a particular implementation strategy and not others. Some students know a great deal, others a little and others still not much at all. Then there is the question of how students relate to the production of public policy. Students might either be proactive or reactive. Proactive students inform public decision-making by anticipating needs and providing public authorities with viable solutions. Reactive students on the other hand do not take part in decision-making but react to decisions, especially when decisions are not student-friendly. Next, there is the question of how students are involved in the process of implementing public decisions. There are two main types of student behavior possible here. Students can serve as facilitators of service or program delivery, such as when university students were co-opted to aid the application of the Operation Feed the Nation program, aimed at achieving food sufficiency in 1976 (Agber et al.

2013, 245). Or students can serve as as inhibitors of program delivery, when, for example, students resisted the increase of university tuition fees in 1978. Finally, there is the focus of the public decision which generates student action and claims. Here also, two general categories of output may spark student activism. The object of student attention might be mono-sectorial (student-centered or revolving around higher education) or pluri-sectorial/ transversal where the issues affect other categories of Nigerians.

Student "agency" in Nigerian universities can thus theoretically either emanate from a full or partial understanding of the issues that generate their activism, be proactive or reactive in terms of how students relate to public decision-making, be student-centric (limited to higher education matters) or be much more transversal in orientation, and have a facilitating or inhibiting approach in terms of output delivery. This is the paradigm I intend to use in my study and it can be presented in Table 5.1.

Before determining which of these forms have been the rule of student engagement in Nigeria, it is important to make a few comments on students' organizations.

STUDENT UNIONS IN NIGERIA

Nigeria's university students are not disconnected from recurrent debates on how best to govern the country. Though they might not be collectively committed politically, in terms of expressed interest in formal politics, they are not at all averse to engagement and are regularly involved in issue-based activism. Such activism is usually spearheaded by representative student bodies.

There are two levels of representative university students' bodies. The first is individual campus-based students' union government. Student unions are established in universities to cater to the welfare of students. Most are founded on principles similar to those I will identify using the example of the Student Union at the Modibbo Adama Federal University of Technology in Yola. The preamble to the constitution of this union clearly identifies a number of guiding principles and objectives. These include the need to protect the rights of students, discharging their civic responsibility as informed members of society and supporting, by all lawful means, the freedom of thought, expression, association, and movement. The union also aims to play a role in the maintenance of a democratic, open, and progressive educational system, ensuring that every Nigerian citizen has equal access to an opportunity to get a decent education. The union wishes to harness the enthusiasm of students for dynamic, purposeful, political, socioeconomic and technological development. It is dedicated to the total liberation of Nigeria from all forms

Table 5.1 A Paradigm for Examining University Student Engagement in Nigeria

		Contribution toward policy-making		*Focus of claim*		*Approach to output delivery*	
		Proactive	*Reactive*	*Student-centered*	*Society-focused*	*Facilitator*	*Inhibitor*
Knowledge of issues at stake	High						
	Medium						
	Low						

of domination and to the attainment of Nigerian Unity and the realization of national ideals. I thus observe that student unions have a broad platform, a multi-sectorial agenda, and the intention to improve on and off-campus social, political, and economic conditions.

Membership of this student union is voluntary. This might be thought to reduce its political efficacy, since this might be thought likely to reduce its legitimacy, for example, by not representing the entire student population. In addition, union activities are closely monitored and controlled by university authorities. At the Modibbo Adama University of Technology, among many of the oversight functions performed by university authorities include the establishment, by university authorities, of a number of quality control measures for those who aspire to be student union leaders, including the possession of a cumulative grade point average of 3.5 and that calls for demonstration by the student body on university, state, and nationwide issues need first to be approved by 51 percent of the entire student body and then afterward by university authorities. Campus-based student unions are governed by a representative governing council or deliberative legislative arm, and an executive board made up of such officers as president, vice president, secretary, and treasurer.

Most student unions can be said to only bark but not bite because of their inefficiency, which is the result of several factors, principal among which are energy-sapping leadership conflicts within them (Uche and Odey 2017, 1–8). Corruption, greed, and embezzlement have become defining characteristics of student union governance in many universities. It is not uncommon for candidates for student union elections at some institutions to seek financial and other forms of patronage from vested interests outside the campus.

At the national level, there is a peak body called the National Association of University Students (NANS). The charter of the association clearly stipulates that the body's *raison d'être* is to express "the position and solidarity of the rank and file of Nigerian students on issues affecting them and the Nigerian people in general" (NANS 1982, 2). This shows that its focus is not singular, strictly student-centric and/or education-ground, but multiple, global, transversal, and society-ground. The aims of the association are thus consequently multi-sectorial, intra-campus as well as extra-campus oriented and have local, national, and international ramifications. Examples of the objectives of the association include the defense of academic freedom and the autonomy of institutions of higher learning, the defense of the rights of all persons to education and work without discrimination in Nigeria and all parts of the world, and participation in the struggle of Africans and other oppressed peoples of the world for self-determination (NANS 1982, 12–13).

The association is a confederation of autonomous student unions which are organized in four zones. Each zone covers a number of contiguous states. The governance of the association is shared by several organs. These include the Congress, the Senate, the executive council, and four standing committees. The two principal organs are the Senate and the executive council. The Senate is composed of presidents of member student unions who have voting rights, and members of the executive council who take part in Senate deliberations but have no voting rights. The Senate approves the budget of the association and is empowered to sanction erring officials and suspend member unions which do not respect their obligations. The executive council is made up of elected officers principal among whom are the national president, three vice presidents (National Affairs, External Affairs, and Special Duties), a national secretary and a treasurer. The executive council executes the decisions of the Congress and the Senate, and represents the views of the association when students deal with the federal government or other relevant authorities within and outside the country.

In liaising with public authorities, the association underlines its willingness to use dialogue and consultation as its modus operandi. However, the association warns that "where the various parties involved are deliberately ignoring these demands, where our avowed constitutional methods of consultation, dialogue, democratic and peaceful means are toyed with, rejected or taken as signs of weakness, the Association reserves the right to enforce these objectives through other means at its disposal" (NANS 1982, 2).

The NANS is thus a non-partisan representative student body at the national level. It is not an "interest group" as defined by Klemencic but rather a "student movement organization." This means that it tends toward "contentious politics and protests as a form of claim making" rather than exist in a mutually supportive, reinforcing, and symbiotic "exchange relationship" with the state (Luescher and Klemencic 2017, 118). The representative student body is therefore not a surrogate of the state. It corresponds to Klemencic's "neo-corporatist" model of students' movements because it is officially autonomous in its operations while being recognized by the state (Klemencic 2012; Luescher and Klemencic 2017, 119–121).

The autonomy of the association is, however, debatable for several reasons. The most important is the existence of the Students' Union Activities

(Control and Regulations) Act (1989) which not only mandated the rule of voluntary membership of students in such Unions but also empowered the Nigerian president, or anyone acting on his behalf, to proscribe students' unions or associations. Student bodies can be proscribed if the Nigerian president is satisfied that these bodies are pursuing activities that negate the "interest of defense, public safety, public order, public morality or public health" or are "illegal, inimical, destructive or unlawful." There is also a senior special assistant to the Nigerian president on Youth and Student Affairs, who is regularly invited to meetings convened by the Congress of the Association and which supervises the activities of the body. However, the fact that the Nigerian state tries to monitor and control the way students' unions operate has not, paradoxically, rendered these bodies toothless bulldogs. Students have been able to air their demands and put their print on several areas of national educational, social, and political engineering, which I now highlight.

STUDENT ACTIVISM

The history of student activism in Nigeria is quite chequered, with many ups and downs involving success stories in student mobilization, leading to the achievement of desired outcomes, as well as failed attempts at claim-making. On-campus institutional and off-campus government responses to student political claims have sometimes been sympathetic and inclusive but mostly not. This explains why most forms of student activism and student power has been contentious. Student participation in university governing bodies is not statutorily provided for or guaranteed. Although many universities provide student representation in committees that deal with student-related matters (Akomolafe and Ibijola 2011), according to Luescher et al. (2016, 22), "In Nigeria, students are not usually considered for participation in the university governing and decision-making; they are only invited for dialogue when they revolt or protest against student policies by the university managers." Thus, unlike countries like Uganda, South Africa, and Ghana where students co-construct responses to student or higher education-related matters, Nigerian students are treated more as outsiders than insiders in institutional and national governance.

Exclusion from the normal processes of decision-making has not prevented students from trying to influence public policy and shape the political and policy process. University students were, for example, involved in the debates that led to the drafting and ratification of the 1979 Constitution which ushered in Nigeria's Second Republic after more than a decade of military rule. Students submitted a memorandum to the Constitution Drafting

Committee, held public lectures, and the president of the National Union of Students, Segun Okeowo, was nominated to take part in the deliberations of the Constituent Assembly which had been set up to ratify the new civilian/ democratic constitution (Ayu 1984, 291). University students gave sustained unconditional support to the federal government in its fight to end the apartheid regime in South Africa. For example, the federal government counted on university students when it organized the Second World Black and African Festival of Arts and Culture in Lagos in January 1977. Such examples of harmony between students' representative bodies and public authorities are, however, few and far between.

In reality, student activism has frequently involved expressions of disagreement with institutional or government choices, usually presented to them as faits accomplis. In table 5.2, I briefly document some of the key manifestations of such activism, from the colonial to the contemporary period, by using the paradigm I developed in an earlier section of this chapter.

A number of characteristics are common to the selected examples of student activism in the above table. All are reactive because students are never involved in the conception of the choices that triggered their claims. This explains why their knowledge of the bases behind such choices is often generally low. The focus of such claim-making is not always student or higher education-centered. In reality, on-campus difficulties appear to be the exception rather than the rule on the agenda of students' claim-making, most of which revolve around more global off-campus conditions of living for the entire Nigerian population. The aim of students' activism is usually policy reversal: students use both peaceful means such as making press releases, engaging in peaceful demonstrations like boycotting lessons, or taking to the streets to mobilize other Nigerians, in order to inhibit and stop the decisions which they are protesting against. The outcomes of such claim-making processes are usually negative because governments typically dig in and defend their preferred policies.

However, there have been some exceptions to this, like the success of the West African Students' Union in combating British colonialism, racism, and social inequalities in West African colonies (Boahen 1994; Peter and Ebimobowei 2015, 385), the success of students at Ahmadu Bello University in Zaria in having their controversial vice chancellor, Ango Abdullahi, fired in 1986, and the success of students, in collaboration with other groups, in forcing President Babangida to vacate his office, following massive protests against his refusal to respect the results of presidential elections in 1993. The outcome in 1993 was, however, equally negative because the winner of the elections, Mashood Abiola, was never sworn-in as president.

I decided to go beyond a simple catalog of expressions of student engagement and to explore students' beliefs about their relations with governments.

Table 5.2 Claim-making by Nigerian University Students and Their Outcomes

Year/Period	*Territorial scope of activism (universities affected)*	*Focus of student claim*	*Knowledge of issues*	*Position of students*	*Students' approach to output delivered*	*Outcome of claim-making*
Colonial period	West African universities	Wide: self determination	Medium	Reactive	Inhibitors	Positive
1960	Ibadan	Defense Pact with UK	Low	Reactive	Inhibitors	Positive
1978	Many	Introduction of tuition fees	Low/medium	Reactive	Inhibitors	Negative
1981	Zaria	High-handed university administration	High	Reactive	Inhibitors	Positive
1984	Many	Tuition fees and scrapping of catering services	Low/medium	Reactive	Inhibitors	Negative
1988	Many	Removal of petroleum subsidy	Low	Reactive	Inhibitors	Negative
1989	Many	Introduction of IMF-backed SAP	Low	Reactive	Inhibitors	Negative
1992	Many	Deregulation of Nigerian currency	Low	Reactive	Inhibitors	Negative
1993	Many	Annulation of Presidential election results	Medium/High	Reactive	Inhibitors	Positive & Negative
2003	Many	Increase in price of petroleum products	Low	Reactive	Inhibitors	Negative

Sources: Etadon (2013), Ajibade (2013), and Aluede et al. (2005).

I did thisby administering a questionnaire to more than 400 students at the Benue State University in Makurdi in 2018. Respondents were both male and female students (75 percent and 25 percent respectively) and included undergraduate as well as postgraduate students (75 percent and 25 percent respectively) drawn from the Departments of Mathematics, Political Science, Chemistry, and Computer Science. Though their views cannot be said to represent those of all Nigerian university students, their responses provide us with some insight into how some University students view their claim-making.

STUDENT ATTITUDES AND BELIEFS

One key question I asked students was if they had confidence and trust in the current political and administrative leaders of the country and if they would be willing to fight to occupy key political and administrative posts in government in order to change the way the federal level is governed or administered. Their responses are shown in tables 5.3 and 5.4.

Two main comments can be made about these responses. First, the link between government and students is not totally broken as half of our respondents claimed to trust the capacity of current leaders to govern well. There is no blanket rejection of the current regime or of its behavior. Second, is the preparedness of a majority of students to join the fray if they could, and take part in the governing process. This means that most students are prepared to be politically and administratively engaged in public problem-solving.

Students were also asked if they thought they could talk about "student power" in Nigeria and if so, what were its concrete or operational manifestations. Their responses are presented in tables 5.5 and 5.6.

Table 5.3 Confidence and Trust in Current Political and Administrative Leaders (N = 420)

Response Type	*Frequency*	*Percentage*
Yes	210	50
No	210	50

Table 5.4 Willingness to Occupy Key Political and Administrative Position at Federal Level to Change Things (N = 385)

Willingness	*Frequency*	*Percentage*
Yes	280	73
No	105	27

Table 5.5 Is There Student Power in Nigeria? (N = 385)

Student power in Nigeria?	*Frequency*	*Percentage*
Yes, absolutely	175	45
Yes, quite often	0	0
Yes, occasionally	210	55
No, not at all	0	0

Table 5.6 Manifestations of Student Power in Nigeria (N = 735) (Multiple Responses)

What student power means	*Frequency*	*Percentage*
Power to force governments to change their policies and programs	280	38
Power to impose items on the agenda of governments	245	33
Power to block the implementation of programs through protests	210	29
Power to generate regime change and to cause the collapse of regimes	0	0

All the respondents believe that it is possible to speak of "student power" in Nigeria, though fewer than 50 percent were completely sure of its existence. What is significant is that none of the respondents believe there is no student power. There is, however, divergence in terms of the concrete manifestations of such power. What emerges from the responses is that students manifest their willingness to influence public governance through some kind of action, as if they were involved in an endemic power contest or flexing of muscles with public authorities. The wish to forcefully generate modifications on government choices or block the application of such choices, corresponds to the reactive and inhibitive modes of operation to which we made reference earlier on in our study.

I also asked students how they view student-government relations today, how they think such relations will evolve in the future and what means they believe students need to use in order to make their claims more effectively. Their responses are in tables 5.7, 5.8 and 5.9.

These students confirmed they see relationships with governments in essentially negative ways and that this is something likely to continue into the future, with a forecast that students may well need to confront government attempts to suppress their activism. Students, however, believe in the efficacy of collective action, through youth associations and student unions, and the primacy of strike and protest actions as the most effective means of drawing attention to their demands and claims. No student mentioned direct participation in formal political activities, through membership of political parties. This confirms that the activities of representative students' organizations are

Table 5.7 Predominant Type of Students-Government Relations Today (N = 385)

Type of relationship	*Frequency*	*Percentage*
Incessant conflict	254	64
Regular Dialogue	70	18
Occasional conflict/occasional dialogue	70	18
Total absence of conflict	0	0
Total absence of dialogue	0	0

Table 5.8 How Students View the Future of Students-Government Relations (N = 385)

Type of relationship	*Frequency*	*Percentage*
Increasingly cooperative and collaborative	140	36
Increasingly conflict-ridden and negative	70	18
Governments will try to control the activities of students and students' unions	175	46
Governments will allow students and their unions to function freely and be a watchdog	0	0

Table 5.9 Means Students Think Can be Used to Make Governments Yield Better to Their Demands and Claims (N = 595) (Multiple Responses)

Means	*Frequency*	*Percentage*
Strikes/Protest actions	210	35
Lobbying	0	
Organized youth associations/students' unions	210	35
Membership of political parties	0	0
Regular press releases	140	24
Collaboration with other interest groups	35	6

non-partisan, a sufficient condition to lending credibility to their demands and actions.

CONCLUSION

The promulgation in 2018 of the Not-Too-Young-To-Rule Act in Nigeria, which reduced the minimum age required to be qualified to run for key elective positions at the federal and state levels, could be read as one official attempt to empower the young in the country and facilitate their entry into key positions of political decision-making. In a country where about 62 percent of inhabitants are below the age of twenty-five, this exercise in empowering young Nigerians may well open up the governing process to direct inputs from young people, including university students and their associations.

My study has shown that university students are not passive bystanders who are disengaged from politics (the term "politics" being used to refer to the authoritative allocation of resources). Although their engagements have been predominantly reactive rather than proactive, constraining rather than facilitative, often oppositional rather than supportive, sometimes unruly and disruptive rather than ordered, students express their interests in how priorities are set, objectives rank-ordered, resources allocated and problems resolved. Students try to count on the political chessboard as much as they can, though in many cases, governmental responses to their claims have been negative and sometimes violent and repressive. Not only are some public choices against which students protest maintained, but theaters of protest are usually shut down and forces of law and order deployed to contain campus disquiet.

Notwithstanding their exclusion from decision-making structures, either at the institutional or national levels, students continue to count on being involved in public agenda setting. Even if they are not co-producers of public policies, they are not passive consumers of such but perform critical evaluative, mobilizational, and agitational roles in the guise of issue-based activism. Because there is no formal representation of Nigerian university students in formal decision-making structures, it is possible to qualify the model of student action in Nigeria under Cele's "non-normative collective student action" (Cele et al. 2016, 183). The focus of students' activism in Nigeria is both "etudialist" and "society-oriented," to borrow two terms used by Altbach as quoted by Luescher (2016, 40). This is because students' union demands "are often directed towards problems of corruption and profligacy of the leadership, economic mismanagement and political mis-governance, the deteriorating living standards of the people and the problems of the educational sector" (Adejumobi 2000, 207). The means used to influence governments choices are usually nonviolent. This includes boycotting classes, issuing press releases to draw the attention of governments, and the public to particular issues, giving ultimatums to institutional and national authorities when the latter refuse to respond favorably to their demands for audience or problem resolution, threatening strike actions, delocalizing the activities of the Executive Council of the NANS to trouble spots (universities, state capitals, etc.) and engaging in on-campus and off-campus protests when all other available means have been employed without success. Unrest and violence thus appear to be a last resort used by students, especially when there is a communication breakdown between representative students' bodies and institutional and extra-institutional authorities. In other words, campus unrest becomes inevitable when both parties not only do not see eye-to-eye, but visibly start talking at cross-purposes.

REFERENCES

Adejumobi, Said. 2000. 'Structural Adjustment, Students' Movements and Popular Struggles in Nigeria, 1986–1990.' In *Identity Transformation and Identity Politics Under Structural Adjustment in Nigeria*, edited by Attahiru Jega, 204–233. Nordiska Afrikainstitutet and Center for Research and Documentation.

Adelabu, Modupe Adeola, and Abiodun Olatoun Akinsolu. 2009. 'Political Education Through The University: A Survey Of Nigerian University Students.' *African Journal of Political Science and International Relations* 3(2): 46–53.

Agber, Tsokura, P. I. Iortima, and E. N. Imbur. 2013. 'Lessons from Implementation of Nigeria's Past National Agricultural Programmes for the Transformation Agenda.' *American Journal of Research Communications* 1(10): 238–253. www .usa-journals.com ISSN :2325-4076. Accessed on 24/03/2019.

Ajibade, David. 2013. 'Students' Crisis in Nigerian Tertiary Educational Institutions: A Review of the Causes and Management Styles.' *Khazar Journal of Humanities and Social Sciences* 10(5): 56–77.

Akomolafe, Comfort Olufunke, and Elizabeth Yinka Ibijola. 2011. 'Students' Participation in University Governance and Organizational Effectiveness in Ekiti and Ondo States.' *American Journal of Social and Management Sciences* 2(2): 231–236.

Aluede, Oyaziwo, Basil Jimoh, Beatrice O. Agwinede, and Eunice O. Omoregie. 2005. 'Student Unrest in Nigerian Universities: Looking Back and Forward.' *Journal of Social Science* 10(1): 17–22.

Amadi, Eric Chikweru, and Cecilia Jabe Ewa. 2018. 'Social Media and the Academic Performance of University Students in Nigeria: A Study of the Rivers State University, Port Harcourt.' *International Journal of Innovative Education Research* 6(1) Jan–Mars: 23–29.

Ayu, Iorchia D. 1984. *Militarism, Student Resistance and the Press in Nigeria, 1970–1979*. PhD dissertation, University of Leicester.

Bandura, Albert. 2001. 'Social Cognitive Theory: An Agentic Perspective.' *Annual Review of Psychology* 52: 1–26.

Boahen, Adu A. 1994. *The Role of African Student Movements in the Political and Social Evolution of Africa from 1900 to 1975*. Paris: UNESCO Publishing, The General History of Africa Studies and Documents, 12.

Boren, Mark Edelman. 2001. *Student Resistance A History of the Unruly Subject*. New York: Routledge.

Brennan, John, Roger King, and Yann Lebeau. 2004. *The Role of Universities in the Transformation of Societies*. London: The Open University, Center for Higher Education Research and Information.

Cele, Mlungisi, B. G. Thierry, M. Luescher, and Teresa Barnes. 2016. 'Student Actions Against Paradoxical Post-Apartheid Higher Education Policy in South Africa: The Case of the University of the Western Cape.' In *Student Politics in Africa: Representation and Activism*, edited by Thierry Luescher, Manja Klemencic, and James Otieno Jowi, 182–201. Cape Town: African Minds.

Cockburn, Alexander, and Robin Blackburn (Eds). 1969. *Student Power/Problems, Diagnosis, Action*. Harmondsworth: Penguin Books.

Eke, Helene N., Charles Obiora Omekwu, and Jennifer Nneka Odoh. 2014. 'The Use of Social Networking Sites Among Undergraduate Students of University of Nigeria, Nsukka.' *Library Philosophy and Practice (e-journal)* 1195. http://digitalcommons.unl.edu/libphilprac/1195.

Emmerson, Donald K. 1968. *Students and Politics in Developing Nations*. London: Pall Mall Press.

Etadon, F. I. 2013. 'Campus Conflicts Involving Students and University Management in Nigeria: The Case of the University of Ibadan.' *International Journal of Education Science* 5(3): 333–343.

Federici, Silvia, George Caffentzis, and Ousseina Alidou. 2000. *A Thousand Flowers: Social Struggles Against Structural Adjustment in African Universities*. Prenton & Asmara: Africa World Press.

Hanna, William John. 1975. *University Students and African Politics*. New York: Africana Publishing Company.

Harbeson, John W., Donald Rothchild, and Naomi Chazan (Eds). 1994. *Civil Society and the State in Africa*. Boulder & London: Lynne Reinner Publishers, Inc.

Klemencic, Manja. 2015. 'Introduction—What is Student Agency? An Ontological Exploration in the Context of Research on Student Engagement.' In *Student Engagement in Europe: Society, Higher Education and Student Governance*, edited by Manja Klemencic, Sjur Bergan, and Rok Primozic, 11–30. Council of Europe.

Konings, Piet. 2005. 'Anglophone University Students and Anglophone Nationalist Struggles in Cameroon.' In *Vanguard or Vandals Youth, Politics and Conflict in Africa*, edited by Jon Abbink and Ineke van Kessel, 161–188. Leiden & Boston: Brill.

Lapidus, Daniela. 2013. 'What is Student Power?' *The Nation*, 9 April 2013.

Luescher, Thierry M. 2016. 'Student Representation in a Context of Democratisation and Massification in Africa: Analytical Approaches, Theoretical Perspectives and #RhodesMustFall.' In *Student Politics in Africa: Representation and Activism*, edited by Thierry Luescher, Manja Klemencic, and James Otieno Jowi, 27–60. Cape Town: African Minds.

Luescher, Thierry M., and Manja Klemencic. 2017. 'Student Power in 21st-Century Africa: The Character and Role of Student Organising.' In *Student Politics and Protest International Perspectives*, edited by Rachel Brooks, 113–128. London and New York: Routledge.

Luescher, Thierry M., Manja Klemencic, and James Otieno Jowi. 2016. *Student Politics in Africa: Representation and Activism*. Cape Town: African Minds.

Lulat, Y. G. M. 1981. 'Determinants of Third World Student Political Activism in the Seventies: The case of Zambia.' In *Student Politics Perspectives for the Eighties*, edited by Philip G. Altbach, 234–266. Metuchen, NJ & London: The Scarecrow Press, Inc.

Mgba, Chimaroke. 2015. 'Civil Society and Democratization in Nigeria: A Historical Perspective.' *American International Journal of Social Science* 4(5) October: 176–191.

National Association of Nigerian Students (NANS) Charter of Demands, Constitution. 1982, 1–34.

N.U.C (National Universities Commission). 2017 Universities' Statistical Digest.

Nyamnjoh, Francis B., Walter Gam Nkwi, and Piet Konings. 2012. *University Crisis and Student Protests in Africa*. Bamenda: Langaa RPCIG.

Odo, Ugumanim Bassey, Felix Onen Eteng, and Maurice Ayodele Coker. 2014. 'Public Opinion and the Policy Making Process in Nigeria: A Critical Assessment.' *Canadian Social Science* (10) 5: 85–92.

Omari, Issa M., and Paschal B. Mihyu. 1991. *The Roots of Student Unrest in African Universities*. Nairobi: I. M. Omari and P.B. Mihyo.

Peter, Zuokemefa E., and Sese T. Ebimobowei. 2015. 'Leadership and Student Unionism, Challenges and Solutions in the Nigerian Tertiary Education System.' *European Scientific Journal* (11), 25 September: 382–392.

Uche, Rachel D., and Edward O. Odey. 2017. 'Leadership Conflicts Among Students on Nigerian University Campus: The Experience of the University of Calabar, Calabar—Nigeria.' *British Journal of Education* (5), 3 March: 1–8.

Zelig, Leo. 2007. *Revolt and Protest Student Politics and Activism in Sub-Saharan Africa*. London: Tauris Academic Studies.

Chapter 6

(No) Right to Protest?

Student Activism at Public Universities in India in the Modi Era

Nisha Thapliyal

INTRODUCTION

Bharat mein rehna hoga, Vande Mataram kehna hoga.[1]
Higher education is not for sale.[2]
Justice for Rohith Vemula.[3]

Since the election victory of Prime Minister Narendra Modi and his Hindu nationalist political party Bharatiya Janata Party (BJP) in May 2014, university campuses across India have been in a constant state of political ferment. Both reactionary and progressive student groups on public university campuses have exercised the right to protest with a vengeance.[4] These contestations underline the dual role of universities as mechanisms of elite reproduction *and* democratization (Kumar 2008).

In 2019, India has an estimated 36.6 million students in various higher education institutions (MHRD 2018) in a total population of approximately 1.3 billion people. Based on these numbers, it has the third largest number of students in higher education in the world after China and the United States. This chapter maps the terrain/contours of contemporary student politics in India around lines of caste, class, language, religion, and gender set within a postcolonial nation-state. I begin with an historical overview of student politics and Indian higher education. Next, I explore the issues and modes of protest that characterize student protest on public university campuses since 2014. I then discuss responses to student protest by university administrations, police, judiciary, and the corporate news media.

The analysis is informed by a range of sources including interviews, activist narratives, news reports, legal judgments, and academic commentary. Readers should also note that most of the discussion focuses on political activism on public university campuses between 2014 and 2019. While dissent has been expressed at fee-charging private universities, it has been quickly and efficiently managed into silence. A recent example comes from Ashoka University where eighty-eight students and staff signed a petition which called for a plebiscite and demilitarization of Kashmir. The controversy that followed culminated in the resignation of two staff members (Indian Express 2016a).

HISTORICAL OVERVIEW

Current campus politics have deep historical roots in precolonial and colonial resistance movements. These roots can be seen in the diverse visions, discourses, and modes of protest that characterize contemporary campus activism. For example, progressive student organizations frame current issues and modes of protest in relation to traditions such as Buddhism, Sufism, and the Bhakti movement, in addition to colonial era anti-caste activists such as Savitribai and Jyotirao Phule, Bhagat Singh, and Bhimrao Ambedkar (AICSS-AIFRTE 2017).

The formal and informal structures and practices that characterize contemporary student politics were shaped by the radicalization of university students during the struggle for independence from the British Empire in 1946. Given the highly restricted nature of access to colonial universities, these students were predominantly male and from upper-class and upper-caste backgrounds.[5] Anti-colonial student activists called for the expansion of higher education as well as the incorporation of mother-tongue instruction (rather than English) for greater access and inclusion (Mazumdar 2019). While some called for unity across cultural differences of language and religion, others laid the roots of an identity politics based on the same differences. Still others were inspired by a socialist vision for an independent India. While an independent socialist strand has virtually disappeared from campus politics, these historical tensions and contradictions shape the political formations we see today in both institutionalized and noninstitutionalized student politics. As observed by Mazumdar (2019), Indian student politics remain an under-researched area particularly in relation to: (a) the mobilizations of the 1970s and the 1990s (see, e.g., Oomen 1974; Shah 1977); and (b) movements located outside middle-class activism (Kumar 2008).

After independence, access to a university education remained extremely limited for historically excluded groups including women, lower castes, and indigenous peoples hereafter referred to as Scheduled Castes (SC) and Scheduled Tribes (ST) respectively. Almost seven decades after the Constitution first mandated affirmative action for these students in public universities, the educational (and socioeconomic) gap between upper and lower castes remains. The gap is so wide that reservation quotas are rarely filled, even with the relatively more recent introduction of different forms of financial assistance for these groups of students. In part, this is due to enduring forms of cultural and institutionalized discrimination and also to a persistent neglect of free, public schools (primary and secondary) for the vast majority of Indian children who cannot afford to pay for their schooling (Thapliyal 2015). The dominant logic of Indian education—"quality for a few"—can be seen at all levels of education. More specifically, the regulation of access to higher education has played a key role in ensuring that upper castes retain exclusive access to the most privileged sectors employment such as the civil service and science, technology, engineering and management (STEM) areas (Vijayan 2020). The recent expansion of universities driven by profit-seeking entrepreneurs has largely failed to expand access. University completion rates for poor SC and ST students as well as those from religious minority groups such as Muslims remain disturbingly low due to pervasive and intersecting discriminations based on caste, class, gender, and language including English (see, e.g., Nambissan and Rao 2013; Tilak 2013).

The terrain is further complicated by a marked cultural shift in relation to university student protests after independence.

Mazumdar (2019) observes that the new political culture attempted to divert student participation toward nation-building and away from politics. While students on the "mainland" could continue to dissent on and off campus, student protests against the Indian state in militarized regions like Kashmir and Manipur were suppressed with a heavy hand (AICSS-AIFRTE 2017). The students of Manipur were among the first to experience the brutality of the 1958 Armed Forces (Special Powers) Act, which allowed the Indian military to act with impunity on grounds of national security. The same policy was also used in Kashmir along with the Public Safety Act to ban student organizations like the Kashmir University Students Union and detain and "disappear" student activists (Pandit 2019).

The terrain of post-independence student politics continues to be shaped by tensions around caste, gender, class, and regional language/identity. The incremental diversification of public university campuses due to a combination of affirmative action and lower costs due to state subsidies has increased participation of historically excluded groups particularly women and students from Other Backward Castes. The All India Survey of Higher Education (MHRD 2016) highlights the dramatic increase in women's participation over the last decade with women currently making up to 46 percent of total enrolments. By law, public universities are required to offer affordable higher education to students from all backgrounds (Chaudhuri 2019), while private universities are under no such obligation. Enrolments from these groups in private universities remain low for women as well as other historically excluded groups (MHRD 2016). Critical and Dalit scholars have long argued that university campuses constitute one of the most visible sites of the expression of dominant Hindu caste privilege and prejudice against lower castes (Teltumbde 2018). Progressive student organizations have become a vehicle for the amplification of feminist and Dalit-Bahujan discourses which speak back to male and upper-caste privilege.

In response, the country has seen an increasing backlash by privileged upper-caste students who reproduce the myth of meritocratic university admissions based on national entrance examinations as well as school-leaving marks. The politics of affirmative action continue to play out around an antagonistic binary: the pursuit of social justice is set against an alleged decline in education quality and/or lowering of standards. To summarize, extent critical scholarship underlines the fact that campus politics were and remain complex. They cannot be simply conflated either with campus-based student union politics or pan-national student organizations affiliated with political parties or with simplistic binaries of Left and Right ideologies (see also Vijayan 2020). Relatedly, public university campuses have provided a home for both progressive and reactionary politics around caste privilege including the rise to national prominence of the ultranationalist Hindutva movement in the 1980s.

By the end of the twentieth century, the Indian state had embarked on a path of slow but steady withdrawal from the delivery of public services including privatization of higher education using the neoliberal rationale of fiscal conservativism. The protection and promotion of the interests of capital by the state facilitated the unregulated entry of for-profit private providers initially in areas such as medicine and engineering and now everything from image management to liberal arts (Tilak 2013). Currently, private colleges are estimated to make up 78 percent of the sector (MHRD 2016).

The Modi Era (2014–Current)

Under the leadership of Prime Minister Narendra Modi, India accelerated the pace of privatization and commodification of education which was initiated in the 1980s by a Congress Party administration under the aegis of the World Bank. Since then, the BJP and Hindu nationalist movement has represented itself as a force of both cultural conservatism and economic liberalism (Hansen 1996). It has manufactured a compelling discourse of development which blends ethno-nationalist and patriarchal versions of

Hinduism, conspicuous consumption, and ruthlessly extractive development (see, e.g., Krishnan 2018). Narendra Modi proved himself to be a master salesman of this discourse of development—first in his twelve-year tenure as chief minister of Gujarat and now as prime minister (Chakravartty and Roy 2015; Vishwanathan 2014).

Higher education reforms have focused on the Sanskritization of university curriculum (Hasan 2016; Kumar 2016) and the restructuring needed to facilitate further privatization. Instead of protesting against the trend to cut the funding of most public universities, university managements have eagerly formed partnerships with the corporate private sector to facilitate so-called public-private partnerships to "upskill" Indian young people. Along with prioritized resource allocation for a few elite autonomous "world-class institutions" (at the expense of the rest of the sector), the central government has withdrawn subsidies and stipends from disadvantaged students, as well as from research and infrastructure development from public universities. Moreover, in keeping with a global trend, universities have adopted corporate management practices based, for example, solely on quantifiable measures like performance metrics of teaching, research and so on (Vijayan 2016). These changes have been accompanied by a shift in management stance toward union activities—traditionally a domain dominated by left economic and cultural politics.

On the cultural front, public universities witnessed a systematic assault on autonomy and academic freedom from the Hindu nationalist movement through the formal policy decisions of the BJP government as well as the actions of its cadres (Sundar 2018; Vijayan 2020). Nivedita Menon, a political science professor at Jawaharlal University was accused of being an "anti-national" by the university administration. While bans on books have always been a feature of attacks on freedom of expression by the left and the right, this practice peaked over the last four years with various books banned for being anti-Hindu and "anti-national" if they were perceived to foreground voices and perspectives of historically marginalized groups like the Dalits and the Adivasis of Central India. The attack on intellectuals and intellectual freedom on campus parallels nationwide efforts to smother the public sphere in a discourse of upper-caste, patriarchal nationalism through campaigns such as beef bans, "love jihads," and *ghar wapsi* (reconversion to Hinduism) (Gupta 2018). Extreme right-wing militants have taken credit for the assassinations of progressive intellectuals including Narendra Dabholkar (2013), M. M. Kalburgi (2015), and journalist Gauri Lankesh (2017).

Caste-based attacks against progressive student activism on public university campuses like Jawaharlal Nehru University, Tata Institute of Social Sciences, and Allahabad University, have been led by the Akhil Bharatiya Vidyarthi Parishad (ABVP)—the student wing of the Hindu fundamentalist organization

Rashtriya Swayamsevak Sangh (RSS) (Human Rights Watch 2019). The RSS provides the ideological foundations as well as the infrastructure for political organization which underpins Narendra Modi's party—the BJP. Known for their violence and bullying tactics, Gupta (2019b, 6) likens this Hindu nationalist youth cadre to "Blackshirts in the academy"—and a key element of "fascist politics" in the country. As shown in the next section, the project of expelling so-called anti-national elements from public university campuses has been undertaken across the country in systematic ways.

In what follows, I discuss how campus-based protests have been in the vanguard of resistance to the nexus of patriarchal Hindu nationalism and the commodification of higher education which threatens to undermine the role of public universities in protecting and promoting democracy (Hasan 2016).

THE RIGHT TO PROTEST

Unrest on Indian campuses has been steadily brewing since the state announced its intention to "liberalize" higher education. For instance, teachers and students protested between 2010–2014 against the unannounced and rapid imposition of a semester system and change of undergraduate programs from three to four years by Delhi University authorities. More changes were announced in 2019 even though educators raised questions about the quality of learning facilitated by these "user-friendly" reforms. As previously discussed, while the acceleration of privatization reforms affected all universities, certain public universities such as Jawaharlal Nehru University were targeted for neoliberal governance reforms while also providing a backdrop for Hindu nationalist identity politics. Suman Gupta (2019b) describes these developments as a "seamless convergence" of exclusionary nationalist and global neoliberal authoritarianism which cannot be understood separate of one another or solely in relation to the nation.

Authoritarian Vice Chancellors

In India, university management structures have always been vulnerable to state control either directly or through the intervention of the police and judiciary (Mazumdar 2019). Higher education scholar Jandhayala Tilak (2013, 6) characterized the system as "highly regulated and least governed." In 2014, the newly elected BJP administration started to replace vice chancellors of progressive public universities with their own appointments. As a general rule, the new appointees lacked any academic qualifications and instead were distinguished by their close identification with Hindutva ideology. Autocratic vice chancellors like those at the University of Mumbai and Hyderabad began to introduce changes with minimal to no due process which affected every aspect of student and staff experience including fees, change of syllabi, and examinations.

These appointments triggered student protests. The most high-profile protest took place at the well-regarded Film and Television Institute of India in 2015. Students went on indefinite strike to protest the appointment of Gajendra Chauhan as vice chancellor—a former actor on television soap operas. He was joined by four other supporters of Narendra Modi and the Hindu nationalist movement—two of whom had no background in media. They denounced student protestors as "anti-nationals" and publicly announced their intentions to "cleanse" the Film and Television Institute campus (Nachimuthu 2017). Their actions received intensive coverage from the national press particularly English-language major television news channels including NDTV, CNN-IBN, and TIMES. The Information and Broadcasting Ministry responded to their letter by inviting students to the capital city Delhi for talks. The strike lasted for 139 days and prompted solidarity protests on campuses across the country.

Neoliberal Education Reforms

Another high-profile mobilization took the form of the OccupyUGC protests which emerged in response to an announcement about substantial cuts in the number of fellowships for master of philosophy and PhD students by the University Grants Commission (UGC) in 2015. The cuts affected approximately 35,000 students who depended entirely on this stipend from the government in order to pursue postgraduate studies. However, the protest received support from all student groups opposed to the privatization and commercialization of higher education. Students occupied the space in front of the UGC office in Delhi between October 2015 and January 2016. Police responded to their march to Parliament with water cannons, teargas shells, and physical violence.

The issue of cuts to funding for public higher education and related fee hikes was highlighted again by student strikes at the Tata Institute of Social Sciences, Mumbai, in 2017 and 2018. The reputation of the Tata Institute, deemed not a centrally funded public university, accrues both from its historical commitment to affirmative action and social justice in higher education as well as its academic excellence (Khan 2018). Protestors highlighted the disproportionate impact of funding cuts on students from groups which have historically been excluded from education including SCs, STs, and Other Backward Castes. In addition to constitutionally mandated reservations, students from these groups have only been able to pursue higher education with financial support in the form of fee waivers and scholarships which have come to be termed as "free ships" (Khan 2018). Activists also argued that the funding cuts targeted three research centers with a focus on oppressed and the marginalized groups. Despite losing the support of the elected student union, activists boycotted classes, blocked gates, *gheraoed* officials (surrounded the premises and blocked entry and exit) and mobilized support from faculty and students in India and abroad.

Repression of Dalit Voices

Efforts by university administrations and right-wing student activists to repress Dalit student voices across India highlighted the contradictions between Hindu ethnonationalist discourses of inclusive Hinduism and the persistent exclusion of Dalits from Hindutva politics. In 2013, right-wing student activists beat up fellow students at the Film and Television Institute of India for inviting artists from the Kabir Kala Manch to perform in honor of Narendra Dabholkar. At the Indian Institute of Technology-Chennai, their complaints resulted in the defunding of a Dalit study group called the Ambedkar Periyar[6] study Circle who organized a beef-eating festival on campus to protest the national ban on the slaughter of cows. However, no action was taken against the right-wing student activists who assaulted and severely wounded Dalit students during the festival. The treatment and eventual suicide of Dalit student activist Rohith Vemula in 2016 inspired nationwide mobilization as discussed in the next section.

Gendered Discrimination

Female students mobilized to resist discriminatory gender regimes that oppress both women and lesbian, gay, transgender, and queer-identified students in different ways. Women (including secondary school and university students) in Andhra Pradesh protested against unsanitary and unsafe living conditions in hostels for Dalit girls and young women, which have led to illness and abuse. Women at Aligarh Muslim University, Benaras Hindu University, and the University of Mumbai also demanded twenty-four-hour library access as enjoyed by male students. Women at the Benaras Hindu University also demanded that they be allowed to eat nonvegetarian food in their cafeterias/messes like the men. Their protests were met with police brutality and harassment but little media attention compared to the two mobilizations discussed next.

Across the country, women under the slogan of *Pinjra Tod* (Break the Cage[7]) protested against sexual harassment and assault on campus as well as restrictive hostel curfews which curtailed their movement in the name of safety. These curfews worked to limit women's mobility in the name of safety and tradition and are enforced both through formal rules as well as moral policing through informal cultural practices which regulate the ways in which women are allowed to occupy public spaces.

In 2014, the #HokKolorob (Let there be clamour[8]) brought the eastern city of Kolkata to a standstill to protest against the way university administrators responded to the harassment of a female student. In the span of a few weeks, the mobilizations escalated from peaceful protests to sit-ins to blocking entrances, hunger strikes, and eventually protest marches on the streets of the city. Activists communicated their demands through public art including music, poetry, satire, graffiti, posters, and social media which Paridhi Gupta (2019a) describes as "highly creative, visible and expressive." Under local and global pressure, the university vice chancellor was eventually and reluctantly removed from his post by the Trinamool Congress administration which enacted a new law in 2017 to eliminate all autonomy for HEIs in the state of West Bengal.

Teaching in English as a Form of Discrimination

Student protests that were largely ignored by national media outlets highlighted a range of factors that contributed to discrimination and exclusion of students from nontraditional backgrounds at all levels of education. The use of English as the medium of instruction has been a persistent source of controversy because of the disadvantages it creates for students who have not experienced high-quality English schooling—a privilege protected by elite private and government schools (Thapliyal 2015). Dalit student activists have long called for more remedial support for students who are required to take examinations in English and/or pass English language courses in order to progress through and complete university. Issues of discrimination and exclusion relating to language of instruction and examination were raised again on campuses in North and South India (AICSS-AIFRTE 2017).

DISCIPLINE AND CONTAINMENT: INSTITUTIONAL RESPONSES

Indian universities have always been spaces of conflict and contestation. University campuses have acted as sites for "unruly subjects" (Boren 2001) and also for the production of disciplined and compliant subjects (Vijayan 2020). Recent student protests on public university campuses exploded in response to the intensification of privatization and authoritarianism in the public university space. In response, the state brought its full power to bear in order to discipline and contain student dissent. At the highest level of government, the protests were framed at worst as "anti-national" and at best as a "law and order" problem.

The discourse produced by politicians, state functionaries (such as police, courts), and allies in the corporate media world always emphasized the "disruption" and "threat" to national sovereignty and pride rather than an affirmation of the role of dissent in maintaining a vibrant democracy. One senior BJP politician and Finance Minister Arun Jaitley labeled student protestors "subversives" and insisted that freedom of expression should be subordinate to upholding the sovereignty of the nation (The Hindu 2017). This kind of discourse normalized and legitimized the use of extraordinary powers to criminalize, terrorize, and silence campus activism including the use of brute force by police and political thugs, colonial era sedition laws, and imprisonment. Rosinka Chaudhuri (2019, 344) reminds us that this was a "democratically elected government exercising power against young students . . . through methods usually deployed against the dispossessed other: the Palestinian, the terrorist, the refugee."

Police Intimidation and Violence

The use of state-sanctioned violence by police on public university campuses across India played a prominent role in institutional responses to student protests on public university campuses. On numerous occasions, university management chose to maintain a police presence on campus to "maintain law and order." In Delhi, police harassed and intimidated protestors including raids on student accommodations. Peaceful marches and protests were met with lathi charges (police charges wielding heavy wooden sticks), water cannons, and other forms of violence. Delhi Police Commissioner B. S. Bassi justified the heavy-handed police response to student protests by telling the media that the student protests were not "an ordinary case [of] unlawful assembly [by students involving] seditious slogans and speeches by certain individuals" (Indian Express 2016b). In West Bengal, the police stood by and permitted political thugs to lead the violence against protesting students, for example, during the Hokkolorob protests at Jadavpur University in August–September 2016. Moreover, female students experienced gendered forms of violence and the threat of violence. For example, in West Bengal and Uttar Pradesh, women who protested against discriminatory rules about hostel curfews, library access, and so forth were sexually assaulted during police action at Jadavpur University and Benaras Hindu University.

Sedition Charges and Imprisonment

Police also used the legal system to silence and punish student activists by using fake First Information Reports prepared by police when they received information about the commission of a cognizable offense as well as more serious sedition charges. Student activists at the Jawaharlal Nehru University (including Kanhaiya Kumar, Shehla Rashid, and Umar Khalid) were arrested by police who used a colonial-era sedition law. The protests in part were held in solidarity with the Dalit postgraduate student activists who were suspended for criticizing Hyderabad University on Facebook. When Kumar was finally released due to lack of evidence, he gave a speech about freedom on the Jawaharlal Nehru University campus which immediately went viral (Kumar 2016). More than two years later, charges are yet to be filed. In the course of the so-called investigation into sedition, Delhi police produced as evidence the following: condoms found in rubbish bins on campus; and a video—heavily circulated by television news media—which was eventually declared to be doctored. Although these student activists were quickly released, this law has become a weapon in the hands of an authoritarian state apparatus to restrict the freedom of speech guaranteed by the Indian Constitution through actual or threatened incarceration. In particular, it has been used to prosecute and imprison activists and public intellectuals associated with the People's Union for Civil Liberties (Shantha 2019).

Judiciary

Events at Jawaharlal Nehru University highlighted the role played by the judiciary in managing and suppressing dissent by historically excluded groups. For over a decade now, the judicial system as a whole has facilitated and supported the neoliberal project for education reform in India (Kumar 2008). A group of lawyers physically attacked Kanhaiya Kumar on the way to his first court appearance resulting in severe injuries. When he eventually received conditional six-month bail, High Court Judge Pratibha Rani[9] began her statement with excerpts from a 1967 Bollywood song about patriotism. She went on to refer to the student protests as an "infection" which required surgical intervention to prevent an epidemic.

Surveillance and Silencing

University administrators have used the full power of their bureaucratic machinery to deflect, discourage (forcefully), demoralize, and silence dissent on campus. In "Stories of Resistance," student activists from across India identify the ways authorities used university bureaucracy to obstruct their protests. University administrators variously attempted to delay or prevent progressive gatherings through added layers of permission seeking or all-out obstruction such as blocking access to venues to hold seminars and conferences (AICSS-AIFRTE 2017). While Students for Society at Punjab University were eventually able to negotiate permissions and were even successful in inviting a banned speaker, activist-journalist Seema Azad, on to campus, this was a rare example of how students outmaneuvered the powerful university administration who were backed by the police and judiciary. As a rule, university administrations increased surveillance of the student body as a whole through the increased use of identity checks (using Aadhar cards), attendance checks, the installation of security cameras, and hiring of more security guards. The gendered forms of this surveillance have been highlighted and critique by activists in the Pinjra Tod movement (see also Sen 2018).

It is in this context that the suicide of a University of Hyderabad Dalit PhD student activist Rohith Vemula has been treated as an "institutional suicide" or a loss caused by institutional lapses and biases (Laxminarayana 2017). While his death received the most media attention, there has been a steady increase in Dalit student suicides since 2008, nine of them at the same university (Sukumar 2016). Vemula was an active member of the Ambedkar[10] Students Association. In response to protests against their activities by the Hindu nationalist student body (ABVP), the new vice chancellor P. Appa Rao suspended Vemula and four other students and removed their access to university accommodations. In response, the students began to live in a tent on the campus. The vice chancellor stopped Vemula's scholarship payments in September 2015 and Vemula took his own life in January 2016. He left behind a letter where he wrote that "his birth was his fatal accident" (Vemula 2016). He argued that a person should be treated "as a mind" instead of a number or an instance of caste identity. A case was lodged against the vice chancellor (and Union Minister Bandaru Dattatreya who was closely involved from inception) but the vice chancellor was allowed to retain his office. In the protests that followed, he not only invited police on to campus to arrest students, but cut food, electricity, and water supplies to the hostels and blocked Internet access.

Corporate News Media

The news media played a significant role in institutional responses to the campus-based protests in major cities which occurred over the last four years. While higher education privatization reforms have always triggered student protests, these protests have rarely been reported in the corporate news media with the kind of detail and level of hyperbole seen in the most recent period. In particular, student protests outside metropolitan centers have been unevenly reported by national newspapers and virtually ignored by television news channels (Singh and Dasgupta 2019). Commentators also noted the hostile reporting of corporate news media toward many of these protests. This is occurring against a backdrop where progressive news media has succumbed to the intimidation tactics of the Modi administration (Chattarji

2019). As media scholars and commentators have noted, Narendra Modi himself has mastered the use of all forms of media to package and project himself not only as the solution to India's problems but also to define which problems matter to India (see Chakravartty and Roy 2015).

Singh and Dasgupta (2018, 60) argue that representations of the 2016 protests at Jawaharlal Nehru University and subsequent protests has transformed the idea of Jawaharlal Nehru University as a university into a "brand label" for an institutional space which promotes "sedition" and "anti-national" activity. For example, right-wing media circulated video proof of seditious speech by Kanhaiya Kumar continuously until it was eventually admitted that it had been doctored. Similarly, media outlets sympathetic to Narendra Modi questioned university authorities about whether Rohith Vemula was officially classified as a Dalit.[11]

Campus-based struggles against gendered violence enjoyed a relatively more sympathetic (though not necessarily nuanced) coverage from national media and even received mention in Anglophone Western media. The dissemination of student activist voices and their demands occurred primarily through social media such as Facebook, Twitter, and Instagram and progressive online news outlets such as The Wire, Countercurrents, Sanhati and others.

CONCLUSION

This chapter explored the contours of recent student protests about issues of institutionalized economic, cultural, and political inequality as well as the responses of political, social, and economic elites to these mobilizations. As previously discussed, higher education has always been in the crosshairs of right-wing forces in India (see, e.g., Delhi Historians Group 2001; Vishwanathan 2000). In addition, international capital lobbied with great success (through transnational mechanisms such as the World Trade Organization as well as local networks) to capitalize on a highly profitable emerging market with an estimated worth of US $115 billion over the next decade (Vijayan 2020).

The common strand that runs across all of these campaigns is that public universities have been systematically targeted again and again by right-wing authoritarian nationalists as well as neoliberals. Another common strand is that these are mobilizations of poorly resourced students opposed by wealthy, powerful, and networked forces. As one stand-up comedian Kunal Kamra[12] (2017) joked, the students who have been accused of trying to "break up India" are the same impoverished students who cannot afford to pay their bills at the university canteens on time.

Beyond these commonalities, student protest has been characterized by a diversity of ideology, membership, and tactics that underlines the complex and situated politics of student insurgency in response to neoliberalism and religious fundamentalism. First, the diversity of ideologies which shapes students' oppositional identities and modes of protest means that these mobilizations can only be loosely referred to as belonging to the Left (Gupta 2019a). Next, in addition to differences in membership in terms of caste, language, gender, and class, it should be noted that doctoral students played a significant role in many but not all of these protests. Thirdly, modes and expressions of collective protests included both traditional protest strategies (such as hunger strikes and occupations) as well as digital and Internet-based communication technologies (see also Bessant 2014). Fourth, mobilizations have differently but clearly been shaped by local as well as global contexts and events with some protests (e.g., #Hokkolorob, Jawaharlal Nehru University) eventually receiving international support from academics and students. Last but not the least, while some of these activists have quietened down, others have somehow found the emotional and material resources to engage in the 2019 national elections taking place at the time of writing this chapter.

To conclude then, this recent wave of student mobilizations highlight how the Indian public university is yet to be experienced as safe or affordable or inclusive by students from excluded groups. These diverse forms of dissent have cumulatively refocused attention on questions about the role and function of public universities in a democracy, and which groups benefit from the assault on public universities, and which do not?

At this particular historical moment, the counter-publics constituted by student mobilizations can be viewed as a refusal to be silenced and rendered invisible and disposable. This is not only a politics of recognition but a politics of the public which exposed the unwillingness of the state to engage with democratic protest (Fraser 1996). In doing so, student protests and institutional responses to these protests remind us that democratization and social justice cannot be guaranteed by law or policy alone but through the active participation of citizens. They also underline that the making and unmaking of the "public" and the "public sphere" is situated, always ongoing and transcends the boundaries of formal political institutions in capitalist liberal democracies (Fraser 1990).

Regardless of the immediate outcomes of these mobilizations, student protests should also be viewed as situated spaces of learning struggle (Thapliyal 2014). Student activist narratives of resistance such as those published in a book titled *New Wave of Student Movements in India* (AICSS-AIFRTE 2017) are replete with instances of learning "for" action as well as learning "in" action (Choudry 2015). In other words, sites of progressive collective activism constitute sites of counter-hegemonic cultural work and knowledge production which by their very nature are embedded with contradictions and tensions (de Sousa Santos et al. 2008). For example, some of the sites constituted by female student activism offer new identities, relationships, and ways of doing politics. In other spaces, activists are yet to devise a politics that cuts across divides of caste, class, gender, and regional language.

Thus, the significance of recent student mobilizations must be viewed in this sociohistorical context of systemic efforts to depoliticize and destroy the public character of the university. As such, they offer us valuable insights into the contingent and situated nature of resistance to authoritarian, neoliberal states, and cultures of governance. These spaces of student protest stand out as places of light and hope in a political climate where few public institutions including political parties and media have dared to confront the approaching juggernaut of fascism.

NOTES

1. If you want to live in India, you will have to be a patriot—right-wing student protest slogan.
2. Left-wing student protest slogan.
3. Dalit student protest slogan.
4. India has witnessed some of the most brutal violence on university campuses since the passage of the Citizenship Amendment Act (CAA) Bill in December 2019, passed after this chapter was completed. Student protests against the explicit anti-Muslim bias in the legislation at Jawaharlal Nehru University (JNU), Jamia Millia Islamia University, and Aligarh Muslim University have been responded to with violence by university administrators and police. In a particularly deplorable incident on January 5, 2020, Delhi police stood by and permitted a gang of fifty masked and armed men shouting Hindutva slogans to enter and assault students and teachers on the JNU campus for three hours. At the time of writing this update and during President Trump's visit in February 2020, Hindutva gangs have been rioting through Muslim neighbourhoods in the city of Delhi for more than four days again with support from Delhi police.
5. However, there were notable exceptions such as the landed peasant castes of Karnataka who were able to mobilize to oppose upper-caste control over the colonial state apparatus and get themselves recategorized in order to benefit from state subsidies and supports including reservations (Kamat, Mir and Matthews 2004).
6. Periyar E. V. Ramasamy was an activist against caste discrimination from South India. IIT-Madras has long been a bastion of upper-caste male privilege and students were allowed to turn the campus into campaigning space for Modi's bid for prime minister in the 2013 national elections (AICSS-AIFRTE 2017). In response, progressive students coalesced under the banner of the Ambedkar-Periyar Study Circle in 2014 and organized events to criticize government policies. In response,

the HRD Ministry wrote a letter to the university administration demanding the derecognition of the student group citing an anonymous letter which accused the group of creating hatred against the prime minister and Hindus.

7. It began at Jamia Millia Islamia University in Delhi and spread through online networks. Representatives of the Pinjra Tod collective have also joined in solidarity with campus protests for human rights, labour rights, and other student demands. They have garnered media attention for traditional and innovative protest strategies including painting graffiti on university walls (Gupta 2019a, 4).

8. The movement borrowed its name from a Bengali song written by Bangladeshi filmmaker Rajib Ashraf (Chaudhuri 2019). It received strong support from the public in Kolkata as well as through national and transnational online networks which contributed to solidarity protests in cities in India as well as the United Kingdom, United States, and Australia.

9. Kanhaiya Kumar versus State of NCT of Delhi, High Court decision by Judge Prathibha Rani.

of March 2, 2016, W.P. (CRL) 558/2016 & Crl.M.A. Nos. 3237/2016 & 3262/2016

10. Dr. Bhimrao Ambedkar was one of the writers of the Indian Constitution and founder of the post-independence Dalit movement.

11. Rohith's mother is officially Dalit because she is from a Scheduled Caste while his father belonged to an Other Backward Caste. The existing system of caste classification inherited from the British has always been contested. In 2012, the Supreme Court ruled that the case of the child in an intercaste marriage would be determined by the circumstances of the family (rather than the caste of the father as has tended to be the practice). Rohith was raised in extreme poverty by his mother. As Rohith's brother pointed out, denying Rohith's Dalit identity would allow officials to avoid investigation under the Prevention of Atrocities Act (Yamunan, 2016).

12. https://scroll.in/video/830681/watch-jnu-students-can-t-even-settle-their-canteen-debt-never-mind-breaking-up-india

REFERENCES

All India Convention of Student Struggles and All India Forum for the Right to Education (AICSS-AIFRTE). 2017. *New Wave of Student Movements in India: Stories of Resistance from Indian Campuses*. Hyderabad: All India Forum for the Right to Education.

Bessant, Judith. 2014. 'Digital Spring? New Media and New Politics on the Campus.' *Discourse: Studies in the Cultural Politics of Education* 35(2): 249–265.

Boren, Mark 2001. *Student Resistance: A History of the Unruly Subject*. New York: Routledge.

Chakravartty, Paula, and Srirupa Roy. 2015. 'Mr. Modi goes to Delhi: Mediated Populism and the 2014 Indian Elections.' *Television & New Media* 16(4): 311–322.

Chattarji, Subarno. 2019. 'Student Protests, Media and the University in India.' *Postcolonial Studies* 22(1): 79–94.

Chaudhuri, Rosinka. 2018. 'Questions of Minority, Agency and Voice: Student Protests in India in 2016.' *Postcolonial Studies* 21(3): 338–349.
Choudry, Aziz. 2015. *Learning Activism: The Intellectual Life of Contemporary Social Movements*. Toronto: University of Toronto Press.
Delhi Historians Group. 2001. *The Communalisation of Education: The History Textbooks Controversy*. http://www.friendsofsouthasia.org/textbook/NCERT_Delhi_Historians__Group.pdf
de Sousa Santos, Boaventura, Joao Arriscado Nunes, and Maria Paula Meneses. 2007. 'Opening Up the Canon of Knowledge and Recognition of Difference.' In *Another Knowledge is Possible: Beyond Northern Epistemologies*, edited by Boaventura de Sousa Santos, xix—lxii. London: Verso.
Fraser, Nancy. 1990. 'Rethinking the Public Sphere: A Contribution to the Critique of Actually Existing Democracy.' *Social Text* 25/26: 56–80.
Gupta, Charu. 2018. 'Allegories of '*Love Jihad*' and Ghar *Wapsi*: Interlocking the Socio-Religious with the Political.' In *Rise of Saffron Power: Reflections on Indian Politics*, edited by Mujibur Rahman, 104–130. New Delhi: Routledge.
Gupta, Paridhi. 2019a. 'Art(s) of Visibility: Resistance and Reclamation of University Spaces by Women Students in Delhi.' *Gender, Place & Culture* 1–18.
Gupta, Suman. 2019b. 'Indian Student Protests and the Nationalist–Neoliberal Nexus.' *Postcolonial Studies* 22(1): 1–15.
Hansen, Thomas Blom. 1996. 'Globalization and Nationalist Imaginations: Hindutva's Promise of Equality Through Difference.' *Economic and Political Weekly* 31(10): 603–616.
Hasan, Zoya. 2016. 'Democracy and Growing Inequalities in India.' *Social Change* 46(2): 290–301.
Hindu (The) 2017. 'Jaitley Call for a Debate on Free Speech.' 25 February 2017. https://www.thehindu.com/news/national/jaitley-call-for-a-debate-on-free-speech/article17368378.ece
Indian Express. 2016a. ''Liberal' Ashoka University Crack Down: 2 Staffers Quit After Signing Student Petition on J&K.' 13 October 2016. https://indianexpress.com/article/india/india-news-india/ashoka-university-crackdown-student-petition-jammu-kashmir-3079850/
Indian Express. 2016b. 'Use of Teargas, Lathi etc Would Have Turned Patiala House into Another Jallianwalla Bagh: B S Bassi.' 28 February 2016. https://indianexpress.com/article/india/india-news-india/bassi-interview-delhi-police-patiala-court-attack-jnu-row-sedition/
Kamat, Sangeeta, Ali Mir, and Biju Mathew. 2004. 'Producing Hi-Tech: Globalization, the State and Migrant Subjects.' *Globalisation, Societies and Education* 2(1): 5–23. https://doi.org.ezproxy.newcastle.edu.au/10.1080/1476772042000177023
Khan, Ajmal. 2018. 'The Cost of Social Justice and the Protest of TISS Students.' *Sanhati*. 4 April 2018. http://sanhati.com/articles/18657/
Krishna, Anirudh. 2013. 'Making It in India: Examining Social Mobility in Three Walks of Life.' *Economic and Political Weekly* 48(49): 38–49.
Krishnan, Kavitha. 2018. 'Gendered Discipline in Globalizing India.' *Feminist Review* 119: 72–88.

Kumar, Kanhaiya. 2016. 'English Translation: Full Text of Kanhaiya Kumar's Electrifying Speech at JNU.' *The Wire*, 4 March 2016. https://thewire.in/politics/english-translation-kanhaiya-kumarselectrifying-speech-at-jnu

Kumar, Ravi. 2008. 'Against Neoliberal Assault on Education in India: A Counternarrative of Resistance.' *Journal for Critical Education Policy Studies* 6(1): 1–18.

Laxminarayana, K. 2017. 'Why Justice Roopanwal's Report in the Rohith Vemula Case is a Travesty.' *Economic and Political Weekly* 52(46). https://www-epw-in.ezproxy.newcastle.edu.au/node/150380/pdf

Mazumdar, Surajit. 2019. 'The Post-Independence History of Student Movements in India and the Ongoing Protests.' *Postcolonial Studies* 15(1): 16–29.

Ministry of Human Resources Development (MHRD). 2016. *All India Survey on Higher Education 2015–16*. New Delhi: Ministry of Human Resource Development, Government of India.

Ministry of Human Resources Development (MHRD). 2018. *All India Survey on Higher Education 2017–18*. New Delhi: Ministry of Human Resource Development, Government of India.

Nachimuthu, Harishankar. 2017. 'Struggle at the FTII Against the Appointment of Mr. Gajendra Chauhan.' In *Student Movements in India: Stories of Resistance from Indian Campuses*, edited by Ajmal Khan, 1–7. Bengaluru: AISS/AIFRTE.

Nambissan, Gita B., and S. S. Rao, eds. 2013. *Sociology of Education in India: Changing Contours and Emerging Concerns*. Oxford: Oxford University Press.

Oomen, Thomas K. 1974. 'Student Politics in India: The Case of Delhi University.' *Asian Survey* 14(9): 777–794.

Pandit, Huzaifa. 2019. 'Schools of Resistance: A Brief History of Student Activism in Kashmir.' *Postcolonial Studies* 22(1): 95–116. https://doi.org.10.1080/13688790.2019.1568171

Sen, Paromita. 2018. 'Surveillance and the Student: Government Policing of Young Women's Politics.' In *Governing Youth Politics in the Age of Surveillance*, edited by Maria T. Grasso and Judith Bessant, 194–207. New York: Routledge.

Shah, Ghanshyam. 1977. 'Revolution, Reform, or Protest? A Study of the Bihar Movement: III.' *Economic and Political Weekly* 12(17): 695–702.

Shantha, Sukanya. 2019. 'A Year Later Rights Activists Accused in Bhima Koregaon Case Struggle for Bail.' *The Wire*, 6 June 2019. https://thewire.in/rights/bhima-koregaon-activsts-arrests-bail

Singh, Mohinder, and Rajarshi Dasgupta. 2019. 'Exceptionalising Democratic Dissent: A Study of the JNU Event and Its Representations.' *Postcolonial Studies* 22(1): 59–78. https://doi.org.10.1080/13688790.2019.1568169

Sukumar, N. 2016. ''Red Sun in the Blue Sky': Rohith Vemula's Utopian Republic.' *Social Change* 46(3): 451–457.

Sundar, Nandini. 2018. 'Academic Freedom and Indian Universities.' *Economic and Political Weekly* 53(24): 48–56.

Teltumbde, Anand. 2018. 'The Education Mantra and the Exclusion Sutra.' In *Republic of Caste: Thinking Equality in the Time of Neoliberal Hindutva*, edited by Anand Teltumbde, 285–318. New Delhi: Navayana Press.

Thapliyal, Nisha. 2014. 'Learning Knowledge and Activism: Introduction to Special Issue.' *Postcolonial Directions in Education* 3(1): 3–17. https://www.um.edu.mt/pde/index.php/pde1/issue/view/7

Thapliyal, Nisha. 2015. 'Privatized Rights, Segregated Childhoods: A Critical Analysis of Neoliberal Education Policy in India.' In *Politics, Citizenship and Rights*, edited by Kirsi Pauliina Kallio, Sarah Mills, and Tracey Skelton, 21–37. Springer Reference.

Tilak, Jandhyala B., ed. 2013. *Higher Education in India: In Search of Equality, Quality and Quantity*. New Delhi: Orient Blackswan.

Vemula, Rohith. 2016. 'My Birth Is My Fatal Accident: Full Text of a Suicide Note.' *Indian Express*, 19 January. https://indianexpress.com/article/india/india-news-india/dalit-student-suicide-full-text-of-suicide-letter-hyderabad/

Vijayan, Prem Kumar. 2016. 'Privatising Minds: New Educational Policies in India.' In *Academic Labour, Unemployment and Global Higher Education: Neoliberal Policies of Funding and Management*, edited by Suman Gupta, Jernej Habjan, and Tutek Hrvoje, 57–78. London: Palgrave Macmillan.

Vijayan, Prem Kumar. Forthcoming 2020. 'Insurgent Subjects: Student Politics, Education, and Dissent in India.' In *The University and Social Justice: Struggles Across the Globe*, edited by Aziz Choudr and Salim Vally. London: Pluto Press.

Vishwanathan, Shiv. 2000. 'Democracy, Plurality and Indian University.' *Economic and Political Weekly* 35(40): 3597–3606.

Vishwanathan, Shiv. 2014. 'Narendra Modi's Symbolic War.' *Economic and Political Weekly* 49(22): 10–13.

Yamunan, Sruthisagar. 2016. 'By Questioning Rohith Vemula's Dalit Identity, Judicial Panel puts BJP in a Spot of Bother Again.' *Scroll*, 24 August 2016. https://scroll.in/article/814774/by-questioning-rohith-vemulas-dalit-identity-judicial-panel-puts-bjp-in-a-spot-of-bother-again

Chapter 7

"They've Completely Criminalized Us"

Interrogating Student Activism in the Tamil Diaspora

Meena Kandiah

INTRODUCTION

In the early months of 2009, hundreds of thousands of diaspora Tamils held protests in major city centers across the globe, from South Asia and Australasia, to Europe, North America, and South Africa. This mobilization occurred as the scale and intensity of the Sri Lankan civil war reached an unprecedented level (ICG 2010, 21–22). Government of Sri Lanka armed forces drove the Liberation Tigers of Tamil Eelam, a proscribed separatist military organization, as well as the 330,000 Tamil civilians within the separatist-controlled areas, into an ever-diminishing pocket of land in the Northern Province. During this period, death, injury, destruction, and displacement were endemic (UN 2011, ii, 2012). As the civil war reached its brutal climax, the newfound, mass mobilization of younger generation Tamil students emerged, specifically those who were born or spent their formative years outside of Sri Lanka. Previous political leadership in the Tamil diaspora was monopolized by first-generation males, namely those born in Sri Lanka and who fled or emigrated as adults. However, shifting political patterns in 2009 saw younger generation women and men "owning" the Tamil liberation struggle by leading and organizing marches, demonstrations, and campaigns (Rasaratnam 2011, 10).[1]

In the research literature on Tamil diaspora activism, the counterterrorism-inspired concept of "radicalization" has been applied readily to young Tamil activists (Oxford Analytica 2009; ICG 2010; Thomas and Bucerius 2017). In its contemporary iteration (popularized in policy, academic, and media circles following the "home-grown" terror attacks in Europe since

2004), radicalization is described as a psycho-social process that can lead to terrorism (Kundnani 2012, 3–4). Younger generation Tamil activism has also been conflated with Tamil Tigers' propaganda and treated as a remnant of the now-defunct organization (Oxford Analytica 2009; ICG 2010; Brun and Van Hear 2012; Hess and Korf 2014). Other responses include the Sri Lankan state's proscription of transnational Tamil diaspora advocacy organizations (Jeyaraj 2014), in which Tamil students played active roles.

While there are more nuanced readings of Tamil student activism (Rasaratnam 2011; Amarasingam 2013; O'Neill 2015), this securitization frame characterizes mainstream research and policy trends in Tamil diaspora politics (and diaspora politics more broadly), which criminalizes and marginalizes actors who engage in homeland political processes and ostensibly threaten national sovereignty and territory (Nadarajah 2018; Adamson 2012). Discourses that emphasize material and ideological support for the Tamil Tigers' movement, and allegations of irresponsible long-distance nationalism and conflict escalation have overshadowed alternative understandings of the Tamil diaspora's wartime and postwar engagement with Sri Lanka. Less well-acknowledged actions include the diaspora's efforts to support the internationally brokered peace process during the civil war as well as relief, reconstruction, rehabilitation, and reform, as part of the overarching Tamil state-building project (Vimalarajah and Cheran 2010; Brun and Van Hear 2012). Tamil diaspora organizations have also influenced international attitudes and actions toward the postwar transitional justice process in Sri Lanka, taking the form of restorative justice mechanisms (Guruparen 2017)—through lobbying governments, legal advocacy, and collecting evidence (Orjuela 2018). Vimalarajah and Cheran (2010, 15) argue that treating the diaspora's continued engagement with the island as "irresponsible long-distance" nationalism is insensitive and erroneous, particularly given the Tamils' loss and concerns regarding relatives, friends, homes, livelihoods, and community.

My research corroborates this view and finds that sections of younger generation Tamils have become emotionally and instrumentally invested in the historical Tamil homeland of the North and East and its people since 2009. At the least, as key stakeholders, diaspora actors should be engaged with in conflict resolution processes and the development of sustainable political solutions in their respective homelands (Koinova 2018).[2]

This chapter challenges the parochial, deterministic, and criminalizing tendencies at work in research and policies engaging Tamil student activism. The chapter begins by historically contextualizing Tamil student activism, before critically assessing the securitized discourses, which treats Tamil activism as "terrorism." Drawing on empirical data collected between 2013 and 2015, as part of a doctoral research project that investigated how and why younger generation Tamils in London were engaging in political activism, the chapter turns to activists' responses to issues of securitization, specifically exploring the ways in which Tamil students contested the claim of terrorism. In contrast to dominant security frameworks that predict and prevent behavior, a symbolic interactionist and social movement theoretical framework and a critical ethnographic methodology are used to understand behavior, illuminate inequitable power dynamics and aid social change goals. Twenty-five core participants (1.5 and second-generation Tamils), who were mostly Tamil students and recent graduates (one-third were women and two-thirds were men) were involved in this research.[3]

In the literature on Tamil diaspora politics, there is a paucity of scholarship relating to Tamil student activism, especially since the events of 2009. This is reflective of the broader body of diaspora politics scholarship, which tends to neglect young people (Levitt 2009). This research is also particularly timely, since the Sri Lankan state is facing ongoing allegations of human rights violations and genocide against the Tamil people. There are also deep concerns about the international community and Sri Lankan state's transitional justice mechanisms' potential to deliver accountability and justice, more than a decade after the armed conflict came to a cataclysmic end (Prakash 2016; Guruparen 2017).

BACKGROUND

The civil war that traumatized Sri Lanka for over three decades began as colonial Ceylon (as it was known at the time) moved toward independence from Britain. Tensions between the two largest ethnic groups on the island, the Sinhalese and the Tamils,[4] became marked as notions of 50–50 representation and federalism were overruled in favor of a majoritarian Sinhala-Buddhist government, which came to power in 1948 (Tambiah 1986, 68).

Between 1949 and the late 1970s, successive Sinhalese-centric governments undertook actions that soured relations between the two ethnic groups, such as colonization projects in the historically Tamil-inhabited provinces of the North and East, as well as discriminatory language, religious, and educational policies (Wilson and Chandrakanthan 1998, 72–73; Wickramasinghe 2014). As Tamils mobilized politically against the government's changes, they were faced with a violent backlash from Sinhalese groups on several occasion that resulted in the deaths of hundreds of Tamils and for which no one has yet been held legally accountable (Kumar Ray 2011, 488–491; Amnesty International 2009). The recruitment of Tamils into the government's security forces also decreased substantially, producing a largely mono-ethnic Sinhalese force. The collusion and inaction of state security forces, alongside Sinhalese parliamentary members and the Buddhist clergy during successive anti-Tamil pogroms, has been well-documented (Fuglerud 1999; Tambiah 1986).

In response to this marginalization and violent oppression, the "Liberation Tigers of Tamil Eelam" emerged in the early 1970s. This political and military organization was established through the Tamil Student's Federation and made claims about Tamil self-determination, including an independent homeland in the North-East of Sri Lanka (Balasingham 2004, 25–26). By the mid-1970s, elected Tamil parties were also advocating for a separate Tamil state, a manifesto that received popular support from the Tamil community (Krishna 1999, 77; TULF 1979). The government of Sri Lanka proscribed the Tamil Tigers in 1978 and as the government stepped up its counterinsurgency campaign, the Tigers retaliated with attacks on government property (Wickramasinge 2014, 298). However, intra-community violence was also pervasive. The Tamil Tigers were responsible for assassinating dissenters, including members of rival factions, academics, journalists, and politicians (Fuglerud 1999). Yet, in spite of violent attacks against the Tamil community, voluntary enlistment into the Tamil Tigers also increased significantly (Richards 2014). Following the anti-Tamil pogroms, an exodus of Tamils also fled Sri Lanka and a quarter of the entire Tamil population are now dispersed across the globe (ICG 2010, 2).

Although there were grave episodes of violence throughout the protracted conflict, May 2009 was a watershed moment during the civil war. The government declared a counterterrorism victory against the Tamil Tigers and it is estimated that over 100,000 Tamil civilians were killed within the space of a few months, with hundreds of thousands more injured and displaced (Vije and Ratneswaran 2011, 1).[5] Credible allegations of war crimes, human rights violations, and genocide have been leveled at the government, including the targeted shelling of hospitals and civilians in a "No Fire Zone," the rape, torture, and execution of captured combatants and civilians, the denial of humanitarian assistance such as medical treatment, food, water, shelter, and clothing and the violent censorship of media and government critics. The Tamil Tigers were also accused of crimes against humanity, specifically, using military equipment in a civilian area, using civilians as a human buffer, killing civilians attempting to flee Tigers' control, killing civilians through suicide bombings and the forced labor and conscription of children (UN 2011, 23–27; PPT 2014). Following the defeat of the Tamil Tigers, approximately 300,000 Tamils were held in government internment camps to screen for potential associations with the Tigers, where ongoing war crimes and crimes against humanity were documented by international organizations (UN 2011, 2012; Harrison 2012), which the government continues to deny (Sri Lanka—LLRC 2010; Sirisena 2016). The government has faced pressure to undertake an independent and international investigation into said allegations (OHCHR

2015) but more than a decade after the end of the civil war, this objective remains unrealized.

In a "postwar" context, the government has also faced ongoing allegations of human rights violations and genocide. In the heavily militarized northern and eastern provinces of Sri Lanka and in parallel with state impunity, there have been reports of state-endorsed torture and sexual violence, coercive birth control measures, landgrabs, harassment, enforced disappearances, arbitrary arrests, and physical attacks against Tamils (ITJP 2018; The Social Architects 2014; ICG 2012). Linked to this is the process of "Sinhalization," which refers to the government's propagation of Sinhala-Buddhist nationalism through political, economic, and cultural practices, particularly in the North and East (Prakash 2016, 102; Guruparen 2017).

Student activism in the Tamil diaspora has emerged against this backdrop. During the final stages of the civil war, there were mass mobilizations across major city centers, including London, which saw sustained protests over the course of seventy-two days and at its height, 200,000 Tamils participating. Most perceptible was the presence of women and young Tamils, many of them students, who were born and raised outside Sri Lanka (Rasaratnam 2011, 8–9).

In response to the massacre of Tamils in the North and East of Sri Lanka, these students were involved in lobbying British and European members of parliament, giving interviews to the mass media and spearheading protest actions, political campaigns, and genocide-related lectures and workshops in universities, with the goal of pressuring international governments and the UN to implement a ceasefire. The establishment of Tamil Student Societies in universities also increased around this period, intent on campaigning on Tamil issues relating to genocide, human rights, and national rights (Rasaratnam 2011).

SECURITIZED RESPONSES TO YOUNGER GENERATION TAMIL ACTIVISM

Oxford Analytica, a global analysis and advisory firm, released a report in response to the mass mobilizations across the Tamil diaspora in 2009. It described young Tamils as the "driving force" behind the protests in the UK and Canada. It also used the concept of "radicalization" to account for this, highlighting five factors. The first factor, "[c]olonial history" refers to British imperialist policies, which it was claimed had sparked resentment among the Sinhalese majority, since Tamils were overrepresented in privileged public services positions. The second factor included "discriminatory practices," such as the government's language, religious, educational, and citizenship policies following independence. The third factor, "genocide myth," is described as the Tamil Tigers' "exaggerated account" of these discriminatory practices. The fourth factor referred to as "diaspora lenses" represents the diaspora's susceptibility to Tamil Tigers' propaganda because of its distance from the conflict. Finally, the report highlighted the role of Tamil Tigers' "autocracy," namely the organization's violent repression of alternative intra-community voices. The report concluded by claiming that "radicalisation is real and extensive in the Tamil diaspora, particularly the youth" and warns that the diaspora may "once again become the locus of funding and organisation for further spasms of LTTE violence" (Oxford Analytica 2009, page numbers unlisted).

Oxford Analytica's (2009) use of the counterterrorism-inspired concept of "radicalisation" is symptomatic of the mainstream radicalization literature that emerged after a series of "home-grown" terror attacks in Europe (Kundnani 2012, 3–4). In a comprehensive review, Schmid (2013, 8) defines "radicalism" as a belief that the status quo is unacceptable and advocating the use of both nonviolent and violent measures to affect societal transformation. While Schmid notes that such actions are typically criminalized, they may also be legitimate in the context of state oppression and international humanitarian law. Radicalism is historically associated with "social progress" but its contemporary manifestations, especially since September 11, 2001, is associated with dangerous and regressive nationalist, religious, and right-wing agendas. Framed this way "radicalization" is described as a psycho-social process that can lead to terrorism via a range of noncriminal causal variables, such as limited education, vulnerability, failure to integrate with host communities, mass media bias, social ties, exposure to Internet sites, religious spaces, and student societies and to a smaller extent, foreign policy. The British government, for example, defines radicalization as "the process by which a person comes to support terrorism and forms of extremism leading to terrorism" (United Kingdom—The Home Affairs Committee 2012, 4).

There are many problems with this conceptual framing. Firstly, "radicalization" is often taken to be synonymous with "terrorism," in which a plethora of variables leads to terrorist activity. Schmid (2013) finds that these variables are inconclusive and that there is no uniform profile for a terrorist. Secondly, the ambiguous notion of "support" for terrorism could entail *belief*, which is not equivalent to *committing acts* of terrorism. Thirdly, Schmid (19) claims that radicalization's "broader application to political activism of individuals and movements in societies where social development is blocked by non-democratic extremist regimes is problematical." In the context of Tamil diaspora activism, students used democratic spaces to express their claims, as Sri Lankan armed forces were reportedly committing acts of genocide, war crimes, and crimes against humanity against Tamil citizens.

The "radicalization" factors outlined by Oxford Analytica (2009) somehow exclude the activists' perspective, thereby avoiding crucial questions about the strategies and motivations of Tamil student activism. Diversions like notions of "genocide myth," "diaspora lenses" and Tamil Tigers' "autocracy" averts our attention from trying to understand this activism, which is a dominant approach in the study of Tamil diaspora politics (Vimalarajah and Cheran 2010). The ICG's (2010) report on "The Sri Lankan Tamil Diaspora after the LTTE," for example, also argued that young Tamils in the EU and Canada were showing "worrying signs of radicalisation" (2010, 22) without defining the term, nor providing empirical evidence to support this claim.

Thompson and Bucerius's (2017) research on Canadian Tamil youth attitudes to the Tamil Tigers also highlights the notion of radicalization and emphasizes the potential risk of radicalization leading to violence. However, emphasizing the role of belief by itself is not a reliable guide to action. In the realm of contentious or extra-institutional politics (including violent and nonviolent action), it is the *combination* of beliefs, emotions, and morals (factors that Thomas and Bucerius highlight themselves) interacting with shifting macro-, meso- and micro-level conditions (such as government policy, social ties, and individual biographies), that spur action (Goodwin et al. 2001). Thomas and Bucerius do claim that perceptions about the Tamil Tigers could change and that young Tamils were well able to fashion critiques of the organization. This suggests that a counterterrorism lens, which complacently assumes a simple causal link between radicalization and terrorism, is not an accurate way of understanding Tamil student activism.

Other responses to Tamil diaspora activism include the government's proscription of Tamil diaspora advocacy organizations working with the United Nations Human Rights Council (UNHRC) on issues relating to human rights violations and accountability in Sri Lanka (Jeyaraj 2014). The government's actions followed the passing of UNHRC resolution 30/1 in 2014, which recommended an international and independent inquiry into war crimes and crimes against humanity (UNHRC 2014). It is clear that Tamil students have played an active role in diaspora advocacy organizations and the blanket proscriptions prohibited Sri Lankan nationals, including Tamil politicians, journalists, and civil society groups working on human rights issues, from being in contact with the newly proscribed organizations (field notes 2014). However, while the Sri Lankan government justified its decision by citing a potential revival of the Tamil Tigers through front organizations in the diaspora, a spokesperson from the UK Foreign Commonwealth Office stated that they were "not aware of evidence that Tamil community organisations currently operating in the UK are engaged in terrorist activities" and "proscription should not be used to prevent or stifle free speech and legitimate criticism" (Tamil

Guardian 2014). This is also supported by the European Court of Justice ruling, which found insufficient evidence to uphold the claim that the Tamil Tigers had the intention to carry out acts of terrorism following its defeat (Delegation to Sri Lanka and Maldives 2017).

The following section uses a social movement lens to explore the ways in which Tamil students responded to the claim of terrorism after 2009. Drawing on Johnston (2014, 24) as well as Snow, Soule, and Kriesi's (2004, 6) definitions, Tamil student activism can be treated as a "social movement" since it encompasses collective and extra-institutional actions, social change goals, temporal continuity and networked groups, organizations and individuals. The concept of "framing" and associated subconcepts are used to illuminate the interactive, strategic and contextual factors, which informed the claims of activists. Frames can be described as cognitive frameworks and the process of framing involves discursively constructing frames, to capture and condense social issues, in order to generate support and mobilize action and/or counter the claims of antagonists (Benford and Snow 2000, 614). I also draw on Edwards and McCarthy's (2004, 125–127) categorization of social movement "resources" and resource accessibility, to show how Tamil student activists were responding to the claim of terrorism.

COUNTERING "TERRORISM"

In 2009, the government cast its military operation in the Northern Province of Sri Lanka as the "World's largest hostage rescue mission," claiming that over 145,000 Tamil civilians were rescued from Tamil Tigers-controlled territory (Ministry of Defence Sri Lanka n.d.). Using the "global war on terror" trope (Kleinfeld 2003, 111), the government framed its military activities as a campaign to defeat terrorism. In a *postwar* climate, the Sri Lankan government has consistently claimed that "hostile diaspora groups" could undermine the genuine effort in Sri Lanka to promote "reconciliation," alongside the continued threat of insurgency from the Tamil Tigers (Sri Lanka—LLRC 2010, 382; Abeyagoonasekera 2015; Tamil Guardian 2019).

The government's diagnostic framing of the social and political problems in Sri Lanka as a matter of terrorism was rejected by Tamil student activists. Instead, activists attempted to neutralize this claim and pursue justice for Tamil victims by constructing a prognostic frame of "accountability," which targeted public (Tamil and non-Tamil) and institutional audiences using various methods such as exhibitions, institutional lobbying, newspaper articles, and discussion groups. Benford (1987, 75) defines these interactive dynamics of contestation as "counter-framing" or attempts "to rebut, undermine, or neutralize a person's or group's myths, version of reality, or interpretive framework."

A network of several Tamil Student Societies held an exhibition entitled *Breaking the Silence* across UK universities. This annual campaign sought to raise and maintain public awareness about events in Sri Lanka. The exhibition posters included allegations leveled against both the government and the Tamil Tigers. Allegations against the government included the "killing of civilians during the 'rescue mission'," the "deliberate heavy shelling of civilians in the 'no fire zone'," the "execution and torture of naked and bound [Tamil Tiger] prisoners" and the "denial of food and medicine to civilians." An allegation against the Tamil Tigers read "Civilians were caught in the crossfire between the [Tamil Tigers] and the Sri Lankan military, where the [Tamil Tigers] used civilians as a buffer towards the approaching SL army." In this way, the campaign organizers proposed that both parties should be investigated jointly: "It is now widely seen that in order to achieve accountability, an international independent mechanism must be implemented, in order to investigate both sides of the conflict" (field notes 2013). This notion of joint accountability also emerged during conversations with the public, the media and institutional actors, often when activists were pressed about the specific culpability of the Tamil Tigers (field notes 2013–2014).

Yet, in the course of my study when discussing the Tamil armed struggle, the activists described its emergence during the 1970s as a legitimate liberation force against an oppressive and racist Sri Lankan government. As one engineering graduate in his mid-20s told me, the advent of Tamil armed struggle, happened only after decades of political struggle:

> If I look back, so, I would see it as the armed struggle was inevitable, coz' it only happened after 40 years of political struggle and I think after 40 years of political struggle its, there's no way that it's not going to happen. (interview transcript 2014)

Some activists also drew a qualitative contrast between the actions of the Tamil Tigers and the government. One medical student in his mid-20s said, "They weren't ruthless compared to the Sri Lankan Government, they were reactionary." He went on to describe how the dominant terrorism narrative, which has been expounded by political institutions and the mass media, has served to obscure what was happening in Sri Lanka:

> We're Tamil Tiger terrorists . . . that's been the dominant representation since the ban . . . they've completely criminalised us . . . they don't think about the worst massacre of this century so far. (interview transcript 2014)

This activist contended that the EU's proscription of the Tamil Tigers in 2006 deflected attention away from what happened during the last stages of the armed conflict, when over 100,000 Tamil civilians were killed by government forces. An engineering graduate in his mid-20s also described how the portrayal of the Tamil Tigers did not take account of the government's actions: "Near the end, the West were portraying them as like this big problem but no one realised that they're a symptom of like a disease in the Sri Lankan state" (interview transcript 2014). In this account, the Tamil armed struggle was a "symptom" of a larger malaise afflicting Sri Lanka, namely violent Sinhala-Buddhist nationalism propagated by the government. Given the government's internationally recognized status as a sovereign power, its obligations to its citizens and the nature and scale of its actions throughout the course of the ethnopolitical conflict, activists contended that both parties were not on an equal footing in terms of apportioning responsibility (field notes 2013–2014).

At the same time, the notion of "inner-critique" or "self-critique" also emerged during these discussions, with many activists eager to evaluate the actions and ideologies of the Tamil Tigers (field notes 2013–2014). A humanities student in her early twenties focused on the politics of denial:

> For me it's not religion, not God. Like, the only way we can move forward as like a struggle, is to accept those things, come to terms with them . . . I mean we can't complain about denial of the Sri Lankan state if we're in a continual state of denial.

Though this activist felt the Tamil armed struggle was legitimate, she questioned the tactics and the uncritical support given to the Tamil Tigers (interview transcript 2014). The medical student in his mid-20s also agreed about the legitimacy of the armed struggle but stated that he was not a "brainwashed apologist" when defending the Tamil Tigers. He went onto say: "I think the Tamil community needs to have an open discussion because we can't move forward without the truth, right?" However, this confrontational approach in making sense of the Tamil Tigers' legacy was acknowledged as complex and problematic, as a humanities student in his late twenties elaborated:

> I think the [Tamil Tigers] made a lot of mistakes in terms of like, the political was never as important as the military and, political was never as mature and intellectual and progressive as it should have been . . . I mean I'm sympathetic and everything but I don't want to romanticise, even though, sometimes do myself too but I hate the romanticisation of the [Tamil Tigers], which is what happens with so many people you know . . . I would rather for us to speak

openly about them . . . I wouldn't feel comfortable speaking openly about them to anyone right? . . . It's complex right? (interview transcript 2014)

Like most others, this activist was engaged in the ongoing task of critically assessing the methods and ideologies of the Tamil Tigers but he indicated that it was not a topic that could be broached easily because of intra-community tensions and the dominant "terrorism" narrative, particularly in an open forum.

Instead of engaging in the difficult task of directly challenging the claim of terrorism, activists attempted to neutralize the claim and achieve justice for Tamil victims by proposing an "accountability" frame, which called for an international and independent investigation into the actions of both the Sri Lankan government and the Tamil Tigers. In some of the existing literature, the younger generation's commitment to international human rights discourses in the articulation of their claims was viewed as an extension of Tamil Tigers' propaganda and autocracy (Oxford Analytica 2009; Hess and Korf 2014). Yet, these findings indicate that activists were pursuing justice for Tamils via international human rights mechanisms *despite* the repercussions that this may have for the Tamil Tigers.

These activists also co-opted "moral resources" such as "legitimacy, solidary support, sympathetic support, and celebrity" from renowned organizations and people (Edwards and McCarthy 2004, 125) to overcome the terrorism frame, which stigmatized activists and detracted from the massacre of Tamils during the final stages of the war. In her study on counter-framing, Gallo-Cruz (2012) writes that the protagonists in social movements compete with antagonists for the same moral resources, in an attempt to generate public and institutional support. During the university exhibition campaign, activists sometimes collaborated with Amnesty International, the eminent human rights organization, which published evidence of government of Sri Lanka war crimes and crimes against humanity. The organizers of the *Breaking the Silence* campaign also invited prominent people to take part, such as the director of *No Fire Zone: The Killing Fields of Sri Lanka* (2013). This documentary won a number of media accolades and was nominated for many awards, including the Nobel Peace Prize (No Fire Zone 2019).

The campaign organizers also chose to use the non-Tamil director in this campaign on the grounds that it made the allegations against the government more persuasive. Activists often discussed how Tamil witnesses, activists, researchers, and journalists were required to work harder to demonstrate their credibility, in comparison to their white counterparts in the Global North. For instance, the phrase "war without witnesses" emerged in the mainstream media in relation to the final months of the armed conflict, despite the fact that Tamil civilians, journalists, and medics collected vast evidences of war crimes, crimes against humanity and genocide (field notes 2013–2014). As a humanities student in her early 20s told me: "There were witnesses, they just weren't good enough for the West" (interview transcript 2014). Activists were therefore conscious of their subaltern position as Tamils, which sparked larger questions relating to race and the legacy of colonialism.

Although activists sometimes liaised with Western organizations and individuals to enhance the credibility of Tamils and their claims, this was viewed as a strategic necessity, rather than a desirable one. As a medical graduate in her late twenties put it:

> If you take a step back and look at where we were in 2009, we were literally terrorists, as in all the Tamil diaspora was considered to be as equal to the [Tamil Tigers] and therefore terrorists . . . to go from there to where we are now, we could not have done that without, or at least as so quickly in five years . . . without mainstream non-Tamil NGOs . . . so ICG, Amnesty, Human Rights Watch, Sri Lanka Campaign, all of these groups have been really crucial in that . . . does that mean that I am completely advocating what they're saying? No. And that's where I think it's really important that Tamils also have an equal say. (interview transcript 2014)

Another engineering student in his mid-twenties also claimed that "white NGOs" and Western media should not have the "authoritative voice on what Tamils are experiencing":

> We don't need other people to speak for us, coz' the other thing we face is external NGOs, like white NGOs or . . . Amnesty or other papers or the ICG . . . who will try and define what the problem is where, we know the problem, we've gone through it for sixty years. (interview transcript 2014)

This activist was troubled by the possible appropriation of the Tamil struggle by white organizations and individuals, which would then become another issue to overcome.

Activists expressed a desire to reclaim collective Tamil experiences by enhancing their credibility, which would subsequently strengthen the legitimacy of the Tamil struggle. One way of achieving this was for activists to advise other Tamil students (via Tamil Student Societies) in their selection of undergraduate and postgraduate modules, courses, and dissertation topics and/or divert their own educational choices toward the Tamil struggle. By branching into disciplines such as politics, law, and journalism or specializing in particular areas such as human rights law, a richer pool of research and expertise could be generated. This self-production of moral and "human resources" the latter defined as "experience, skills and expertise" (Edwards and McCarthy 2004, 127) would allow activists to take ownership of the issues which affected their community, without having to rely on white individuals and organizations from the Global North and, in addition, counter the claims of the Sri Lankan government and other antagonists (field notes 2013–2014).

CONCLUSION

Despite the defeat of the Tamil Tigers over a decade ago, counterterrorism discourses prevail in the context of Tamil diaspora activism. This chapter challenged the way analysts and state actors deployed the language of "terrorism" in relation to Tamil student activism. The idea of "radicalization" emerged that as a counterterrorism concept is preoccupied with identifying the noncriminal causal factors (including political activism), which could lead to terrorism. Yet, its explanatory power is weak and there are problems in its conceptualization, which confuses political beliefs with the propensity to commit acts of terrorism. Citing a potential resurgence of Tamil Tigers' violence, the Sri Lankan government also proscribed a vast number of diaspora advocacy organizations that Tamil students were working with. Rather than reflecting legitimate concerns about the revival of the Tamil Tigers, these actions have deliberate and far-reaching consequences in terms of investigating state war crimes and ongoing crimes against humanity and genocide, as well as developing sustainable political solutions in Sri Lanka.

The latter half of the chapter documented some of the ways Tamil student activists set about strategically countering the pervasive claim of terrorism. In their activism, Tamil students constructed an "accountability" frame, which proposed a joint international and independent investigation of both Sri Lankan government and Tamil Tigers' actions during the course of the armed conflict. Activists counter-balanced allegations of terrorism through their commitment to international human rights mechanisms. This contradicts some of the existing literature, which saw Tamil students' utilization of international human rights discourses, as an extension of Tamil Tigers' propaganda and autocracy. Despite agreeing about the legitimacy of the armed struggle, many activists were also engaged in the ongoing task of critically evaluating the Tamil Tigers' ideologies and methods, though this was limited to and within intra-community settings, due to its complexity and the dominant terrorism narrative. Conscious of their marginal and criminalized status as Tamils, student activists also reluctantly borrowed "moral resources" from well-known human rights organizations and white individuals in the Global North to support their claims. However, they were also in the process of self-producing moral and human resources within the

Tamil student community, by selecting particular modules, courses, and dissertation topics at universities, that is related to the Tamil struggle. Thus, instead of the continued marginalization and criminalization of younger generation Tamil activists, given their commitment and capacity, meaningful collaborations between activists, analysts, and state actors are necessary in the context of conflict resolution processes in Sri Lanka.

NOTES

1. "Younger generation Tamil activism" and "Tamil student activism" are used interchangeably in this chapter, since the former incorporates the latter and much of the existing literature makes little distinction between the two.
2. In this chapter, diasporas are considered to be "discursively constructed" rather than "natural entities" (Adamson 2012, 29) and includes "those who are mobilized to engage in homeland political processes" (Lyons and Mandaville 2010, 126).
3. "1.5 generation" refers to participants who left their country of origin as children (in this study, approximately before the age of twelve) and spent their formative years elsewhere (in this study, at least ten years were spent living outside the country of origin) (Brun and Van Hear 2012). "Second generation" refers to participants who were born outside of their parents' country of origin (Ramakrishnan 2004).
4. "Tamils" are distinguished from other ethnically divergent Tamil-speaking communities in Sri Lanka, such as Muslim and Malayagam Tamils.
5. Some estimates place the death toll at over 100,000 (Prakash 2016, 93). The International Truth and Justice Project are currently in the process of "counting the dead" (ITJP n.d.).

REFERENCES

Abeyagoonasekera, Asanga. 2015. 'Threats to Sri Lanka After Ending Insurgency and Terrorism.' *Colombo Telegraph*, 10 May 2015. https://www.colombotelegraph.com/index.php/threats-to-sri-lanka-after-ending-insurgency-terrorism/.

Adamson, Fiona B. 2012. 'Constructing the Diaspora: Diaspora Identity Politics and Transnational Social Movements.' In *Politics from Afar: Transnational Diaspora Networks*, edited by Terrence Lyons and Peter Mandaville, 25–44. New York: Colombia University Press.

Amarasingam, Amarnath. 2013. *A History of Tamil Diaspora Politics in Canada: Organisational Dynamics and Negotiated Order, 1978–2013.* International Centre for Ethnic Studies, Research Paper No. 11. https://www.academia.edu/5458036/A_History_of_Tamil_Diaspora_Politics_in_Canada_ Organisational_Dynamics_and_Negotiated_Order_1978-2013.

Amnesty International. 2009. *Twenty Years of Make-Believe: Sri Lanka.* http://www.observatori.org/paises/pais_75/documentos/srilanka.pdf.

Balasingham, Anton. 2004. *War and Peace: Armed Struggle and Peace Efforts of Liberation Tigers*. England: Fairmax Publishing Ltd.
Benford, Robert D. 1987. *Framing Activity, Meaning, and Social Movement Participation: The Nuclear Disarmament Movement*. PhD Thesis, University of Texas.
Benford, Robert D., and David A. Snow. 2000. 'Framing Processes and Social Movements: An Overview and Assessment.' *Annual Review of Sociology* 26, no. 1: 611–639.
Brun, Cathrine, and Nicholas Van Hear. 2012. 'Between the Local and the Diasporic: The Shifting Centre of Gravity in War-Torn Sri Lanka's Transnational Politics.' *Contemporary South Asia* 20, no. 1: 61–75.
Delegation to Sri Lanka and Maldives. 2017. *Statement on the Judgement Relating to the LTTE by the European Court of Justice*. Colombo. https://eeas.europa.eu/delegations/sri-lanka_en/30471/Statement%20on%20the%20judgement%20relating%20to%20the%20LTTE%20by%20the%20European%20Court%20of%20Justice.
Edwards, Bob, and John D. McCarthy. 2004. 'Resources and Social Movement Mobilization.' In *The Blackwell Companion to Social Movements*, edited by David A. Snow, Sarah Soule, and Hanspeter Kriesi, 116–152. Malden: Blackwell.
Fuglerud, Øivind. 1999. *Life on the Outside: The Tamil Diaspora and Long-Distance Nationalism*. London: Pluto.
Gallo-Cruz, Selina. 2012. 'Negotiating the Lines of Contention: Counterframing and Boundary Work in the School of the Americas Debate.' *Sociological Forum* 27, no. 1: 21–45.
Goodwin, Jeff, James M. Jasper, and Francesca Polletta. 2001. *Passionate Politics: Emotions and Social Movements*. London: The University of Chicago Press.
Guruparen. K. 2017. 'The Politics of the Discourse on Post-War Reconciliation in Sri Lanka: Some Preliminary Notes.' In *Sri Lanka: The Struggle for Peace in the Aftermath of War*, edited by Amarnath Amarasingam and Daniel Bass, 15–34. London: Hurst.
Harrison, Francis. 2012. *Still Counting the Dead: Survivors of Sri Lanka's Hidden War*. London: Portobello Books.
Hess, Monika, and Benedikt Korf. 2014. 'Tamil Diaspora and the Political Spaces of Second-Generation Activism in Switzerland.' *Global Networks* 14, no. 4: 419–437.
Home Affairs Committee (UK). 2012. *Roots of Violent Radicalisation: Nineteenth Report of Session 2010–2012*. Volume 1. London: The Stationary Office Limited.
ICG (International Crisis Group). 2010. *The Sri Lankan Tamil Diaspora After the LTTE*. https://d2071andvip0wj.cloudfront.net/186-the-sri-lankan-tamil-diaspora-after-the-ltte.pdf.
ICG (International Crisis Group). 2012. *Sri Lanka's North II: Rebuilding Under the Army*. https://d2071andvip0wj.cloudfront.net/220-sri-lanka-s-north-ii-rebuilding-under-the-military.pdfunder-the-military.pdf.
ITJP (International Truth and Justice Project). 2018. *Ongoing Torture*. http://www.itjpsl.com/assets/ITJP_ongoing_violations_fact_sheet_v6.1.pdf.
ITJP (International Truth and Justice Project). n.d. *Counting the Dead*. Accessed 1 June 2019. http://www.itjpsl.com/reports/counting-the-dead.

Jeyaraj, David B. S. 2014. *Sri Lanka Proscribes 15 Suspected LTTE Front Organizations Abroad as Foreign Terrorist Entities Under UN Resolution 1373.* DBSJeyaraj.com. http://dbsjeyaraj.com/dbsj/archives/29147.

Johnston, Hank. 2014. *What is a Social Movement?* Cambridge: Polity.

Kleinfeld, Margo. 2003. 'Strategic Troping in Sri Lanka: September Eleventh and the Consolidation of Political Position.' *Geopolitics* 8, no. 3: 105–126.

Koinova, Maria. 2018. 'Diaspora Mobilisation for Conflict and Post-Conflict Reconstruction: Contextual and Comparative Dimensions.' *Journal of Ethnic and Migration Studies* 44, no. 8: 1251–1269.

Krishna, Sankaram. 1999. *Postcolonial Insecurities: India, Sri Lanka, and the Question of Nationhood.* Minneapolis: University of Minnesota Press.

Kumar Ray, Jayanta. 2011. *India's Foreign Relations, 1947–2007.* New Delhi: Routledge.

Kundnani, Arun. 2012. 'Radicalisation: The Journey of a Concept.' *Race and Class* 54, no. 2: 3–25.

Levitt, Peggy. 2009. 'Roots and Routes: Understanding the Lives of the Second Generation Transnationality.' *Journal of Ethnic and Migration Studies* 35, no. 7: 1225–1224.

Lyons, Terrence, and Peter Mandaville. 2010. 'Think Locally, Act Globally: Toward a Transnational Comparative Politics.' *International Political Sociology* 4, no. 22: 124–121.

Ministry of Defence Sri Lanka. n.d. *World's Largest Hostage Rescue Mission Becomes Success.* Accessed 1 June 2019. http://www.defence.lk/hm/hm.asp.

Nadarajah, Suthaharan. 2018. 'The Tamil Proscriptions: Identities, Legitimacies, and Situated Practices.' *Terrorism and Political Violence* 30, no. 2: 278–297.

No Fire Zone. 2013. *Directed by Callum Macrae.* UK: Outsider Films.

No Fire Zone. 2019. *Awards and Reviews.* https://nofirezone.org/reviews—awards.

OHCHR (Office of the United Nations High Commissioner for Human Rights). 2015. *Comprehensive Report of the Office of the United Nations High Commissioner for Human Rights on Sri Lanka.* A/HRC/30/61. http://www.ohchr.org/EN/NewsEvents/Pages/DisplayNews.aspx?NewsID=16432&LangI D=E.

O'Neill, Tom. 2015. 'In the Path of Heroes: Second-Generation Tamil-Canadians After the LTTE.' *Identities: Global Studies in Culture and Power* 22, no. 1: 124–139.

Orjuela, Camilla. 2018. 'Mobilising Diasporas for Justice. Opportunity Structures and the Presencing of a Violent Past.' *Journal of Ethnic and Migration Studies* 44, no. 8: 1357–1373.

Oxford Analytica. 2009. *Sri Lanka: Radical Diaspora Could Back New Violence.* http://reliefweb.int/report/sri-lanka/sri-lanka-radical-diaspora-could-back-newviolence.

PPT (Permanent Peoples' Tribunal). 2014. *Permanent Peoples' Tribunal on Sri Lanka.* http://permanentpeoplestribunal.org/wp-content/uploads/2014/01/Sentenza-Sri-Lanka-and-Tamil-II.pdf.

Prakash, Vinay. 2016. 'Sri Lanka.' In *Redefining Genocide: Settler Colonialism, Social Death and Ecocide*, edited by Damien Short, 93–126. London: Zed Books.

Ramakrishnan, Karthick S. 2004. 'Second Generation Immigrants? The 2.5 Generation in the United States.' *Social Science Quarterly* 85, no. 2: 380–399.

Rasaratnam, Madura. 2011. *Political Identity of the British Tamil Diaspora: Implications for Engagement.* Berghof Peace Support and Centre for Just Peace and Democracy. http://elibrary.humanitariansrilanka.org/wp-content/uploads/2016/11/SL_Diaspora_Papers_-madurika-Rasaratnam.pdf.

Richards, Joanne. 2014. *An Institutional History of the Liberation Tigers of Tamil Eelam LTTE.* The Centre for Conflict, Development and Peacebuilding, Working Paper 10. http://repository.graduateinstitute.ch/record/292651/files/CCDP-Working-Paper-10-LTTE-1.pdf.

Schmid, Alex P. 2013 *Radicalisation, De-Radicalisation, Counter-Radicalisation: A Conceptual Discussion and Literature Review.* International Centre for Counter-Terrorism—The Hague. https://www.icct.nl/download/file/ICCT-Schmid-Radicalisation-De-Radicalisation-Counter-Radicalisation-March-2013.pdf.

Sirisena, Maithripala. 2016. 'Talk to Al Jazeera.' Interview by Hoda Abdel-Hamid. *Al Jazeera*, 29 January 2016.

Snow, David A., Sarah A. Soule, and Hanspeter Kriesi. 2004. *The Blackwell Companion to Social Movements.* Malden, MA: Blackwell.

Sri Lanka—LLRC (Lessons Learnt and Reconciliation Commission). 2010. *Report of the Commission of Inquiry on Lessons Learnt and Reconciliation. P.O. No. CA/3/3/24.* Colombo.

Tambiah, Stanley. 1986. *Sri Lanka: Ethnic Fratricide and the Dismantling of Democracy.* Chicago: University Chicago Press.

Tamil Guardian. 2014. 'Diaspora Orgs Proscription Should Not Be Used to Stifle Free Speech and Legitimate Criticism, UK Tells Sri Lanka.' *Tamil Guardian*, 1 April 2014. https://www.tamilguardian.com/content/diaspora-orgs-proscription-should-not-be-used-stifle-free-speech-and-legitimate-criticism-uk.

Tamil Guardian. 2019. 'British Counter-Terror Police Arrest 'Sri Lankan' Nationals at UK Airport.' *Tamil Guardian*, 13 April 2019. https://www.tamilguardian.com/content/british-counter-terror-police-arrest-%E2%80%98sri-lankan-nationals%E2%80%99-uk-airport.

The Social Architects. 2014. *Coercive Population Control in Kilinochchi.* http://www.tsasouthasia.org/eng/articles/coercive-population-control-in-kilinochchi/.

Thomas, Sara K., and Sandra M. Bucerius. 2017. 'Transnational Radicalization, Diaspora Groups, and Within-Group Sentiment Pools: Young Tamil and Somali Canadians on the LTTE and Al Shabaab.' *Terrorism and Political Violence* 31, no. 3: 1–18. https://www.tandfonline.com/doi/abs/10.1080/09546553.2016.1264938?journalCode=ftpv20.

TULF (Tamil United Liberation Front). 1976. *Vaddukoddai Resolution.* Ilankai Tamil Sangam. http://www.sangam.org/FB_HIST_DOCS/vaddukod.htm.

UN. 2011. *Report of the Secretary-General's Panel of Experts on Accountability in Sri Lanka.* http://www.un.org/News/dh/infocus/Sri_Lanka/POE_Report_Full.pdf.

UN. 2012. *Report of the Secretary General's Internal Review Panel on United Nations Action in Sri Lanka.* http://www.un.org/News/dh/infocus/Sri_Lanka/The_Internal_Review_Panel_report_on_Sri_Lanka.pdf.

UNHRC (United Nations Human Rights Council). 2014. *Promoting reconciliation, accountability and human rights in Sri Lanka*. A/HRC/RES/25/1. https://documents-dds-ny.un.org/doc/UNDOC/GEN/G14/132/86/PDF/G1413286.pdf?OpenElement.

Vije, Mayan, and Suppiah Ratneswaran. 2011. *War Crimes and Crimes Against Humanity in Sri Lanka: Chronology of Events September 2008—January 2010.* Kingston-Upon-Thames: Tamil Information Centre.

Vimalarajah, Lukshi, and R. Cheran. 2010. *Empowering Diasporas: The Dynamics of Post-war Transnational Tamil Politics*. Berghof Occasional Paper No. 31. Berghof Peace Support. http://www.berghof-foundation.org/fileadmin/redaktion/Publications/Papers/Occasional_Papers/boc31eBPS.pdf.

Wilson, Alfred J., and A. Joseph Chandrakanthan. 1998. *Tamil Identity and Aspirations*. Conciliation Resources: Working Together for Peace. http://www.c-r.org/accord/sri-lanka/tamil-identity-and-aspirations.

Chapter 8

#yosoy132

Indignation, Information, and Pro-Democracy Activism in Mexico, 2011–2012

Lorna Zamora Robles

INTRODUCTION

#yosoy132 was a social movement led and mobilized by students in Mexico that was active between 2012 and 2013. It attracted a wide base of support throughout the country during the 2012 federal elections and beyond. The nonviolent movement called for the democratization of the media and protection of the right to free speech. With democracy at the core of the movement, the movement's participants rejected traditional modes of leadership and hierarchical decision-making processes, preferring to use more horizontal procedures.

Nearly a decade after the #yosoy132 movement uprisings, questions about its significance are still being assessed. #yosoy132 offered its participants a space for hope, resistance, and learning. In this chapter, I discuss the contribution of #yosoy132, reflecting on the lessons learned from it and assessing its relationship with other social movements.

In 2011–2012, I was an undergraduate student in the Faculty of Philosophy and Literature of Universidad Nacional Autónoma de México (UNAM). A great proportion of students in the faculty had traditionally been involved in a number of social justice movements. In this environment, I was active in other political organizations so when #yosoy132 sprouted, I quickly became engaged in the discussions, organizational activities, and protest actions (demonstrations).

Here in this chapter, I draw on a mix of social movement theory and documents produced by other participants of Yo Soy 132. Accounts of the events and the media response to it have been documented, among others, by Morales (2014) and Galindo Cáceres and González-Acosta (2013). I also draw on my own experiences and discussions with fellow students and demonstrators since 2011. I offer some reflections on my own experience of the events, as well as the social and internal processes of the movement that took place between May and December 2012.

I begin with the Mexican political context to situate the movement. I then discuss how the movement began and present the role of students in it. I also highlight the influence of social media in the movement, both as its enabler and as integral to its demands. Attention is then given to the actions and principles of the movement, especially its theory of nonviolent action. I discuss the responses of the media, society, and state, drawing on Weber's account of the state and the legitimate use of "force" (*gewalt*). I do this to question whether the use of violence by the Mexican state was legitimate. Finally, I look at the legacy of the movement in terms of options to escape the current ways of politics, media, and participation in Mexico.

MEXICAN POLITICS IN 2012: THE RETURN OF THE DINOSAUR

A presidential election was due to take place in Mexico on July 1, 2012. There were three major candidates running for office: Josefina Vázquez Mota from Partido Acción Nacional (PAN), Andrés Manuel López Obrador from Partido de la Revolución Democrática (PRD), and Enrique Peña Nieto from Partido Revolucionario Institucional (PRI). Opinion polls projected a slight advantage for Peña Nieto over Andrés Manuel López Obrador from the left. By May 2012, just a couple of months before the election, the presidential race was tight and many voters were still undecided (*Animal Político* 2012a).

PAN, the right-wing party, had won the presidential election in 2000, in a so-called transition to democracy after seventy years of rule by the centralist PRI. In 2012, PAN was about to complete a controversial term encompassing a questionable security strategy: President Felipe Calderón's "War on Drugs" ended the six years of his mandate with thousands of displaced, murdered, and disappeared persons.

López Obrador, Partido de la Revolución Democratica's candidate, had previously run for presidency in 2006, losing to Felipe Calderón in an election that many believed was fraudulent (El País 2006). In a highly controversial move, López Obrador and his supporters blocked Reforma Avenue, the center of Mexico City's financial district, for several months. By exposing corruption, López Obrador was considered by some to be a symbol of democracy, though for others, his lack of acceptance of the official results and institutions posed a threat.

In the 2012 electoral campaign, the former governor of the state of Mexico and the PRI's presidential candidate, Enrique Peña Nieto, received a lot of media coverage. Televisa, a major television broadcaster, represented him, for example, as a young, promising liberal politician. His marriage to Angélica Rivera, a soap-opera actress who starred in his campaign advertisements, attracted a lot of media coverage. Social justice movements and certain elements of the press drew attention to his role in the Atenco case.

Indeed, during Peña Nieto's term as governor, the town of San Salvador Atenco was terrorized by the police, whose officers had killed two people, and raped and tortured eleven women (Rojas 2018). The Atenco case was an example of state repression under a PRI government as its normal *modus operandi*. During its seventy years of leadership in national government, many cases of state-sponsored violence were documented, including the Aguas Blancas Massacre, the Acteal Massacre, and the Tlatelolco Massacre. The PRI was colloquially referred to as *the dinosaur* ("el dinosaurio"), partly due to its institutional stability and partly because of the predatory characteristics of the people who held power in it for such a long time. The return of the PRI to the presidency would mean, to many, the return of bad old practices.

EMERGENCE OF YO SOY 132: YOUNG PEOPLE AND POLITICAL PARTICIPATION

On May 11, 2012, Peña Nieto gave a speech at the Universidad Iberoamericana, a private Jesuit university in Mexico City, as a part of the *Good Citizen Forum*. Peña Nieto refused to answer questions about the Atenco case, or about his campaign expenses, which had used public funds. Faced with a spontaneous demonstration of disapproval, Peña Nieto left the room. Politicians from his party and media coverage later argued that the "left-wing party" had infiltrated the event with agitators, as it was impossible that the "upper-class university students" who attended the Universidad Iberoamericana would cause such a scandal. The PRI, backed by the media, tried to silence the students' voices by minimizing what had happened. This fueled students' anger, providing evidence for the kind of censorship practices that a PRI government would employ (Galindo Cáceres and González-Acosta 2013, 82).

A few days later, a video was broadcast on YouTube. It showed the 131 students who were at the forum and their university identification cards, proving they were indeed students and were against Peña Nieto (*Vapormipatria* 2012). The hashtag #yosoy132, *I am student 132*, became a Twitter trending meme, attracting people who were not at the event but supported the demonstrators. The movement grew quickly, with massive demonstrations taking place in Mexico City and other parts of the country.

I remember the first massive demonstrations of Yo Soy 132 in the Zócalo, the main square of Mexico City. Everywhere I looked, the streets were flooded with people. I felt full of life and energy. Something important was happening and that change was in the air. I felt the rush of the chants and the steps of tens of thousands of people who were as fed up as I was with injustice, corruption, and a fraudulent political regime where everything seemed to be prearranged and where we had no space. I felt like I was part of something bigger than myself, a *we*. And what we were feeling was hope.

The massive demonstrations nurtured a feeling of unity. Not only was it refreshing to see that apathy and cynicism were far from being real, but also to see how many others shared this anger and eagerness for change. While walking side by side with so many people, our confrontation of our fears of not being heard, of being repressed, of being silenced, and of having our message misrepresented was a profoundly transformative moment. As a group, being together in an environment of fellowship gave us strength. Our fears could have manifested into reality, but we were supported by the group. It would have not been as easy to silence us all, and if they hurt somebody the rest would show up in solidarity in other parts of the country.

In Latin America, students have historically been central to social justice movements. Nevertheless, following the 1999 general strike at UNAM, students were represented as "apolitical," "skeptical," and somewhat feckless, lacking any real interest in mobilizing (Ortega Olivares 2010). There was a widespread prejudice that student demonstrators were "lazy," "disgruntled" people largely drawn from the lower classes with nothing much to do but destabilize the government.

In 2011, many students who joined the #yosoy132 demonstrations were drawn from middle- or upper-middle classes, belonging to private universities like Universidad Iberoamericana (IBERO), Instituto Tecnológico y de Estudios Superiores de Monterrey (ITESM), and Instituto Tecnológico Autónomo de México (ITAM), which had not been noticeably active in previous political demonstrations and social actions. They now believed that their rights had been directly infringed. Their subsequent mobilization rejected the older stereotypes of student protesters reproduced by center and right-wing advocates, which gave even wider visibility to #yosoy132.

The contact among such diverse participants of the movement helped challenge the stereotypes of people from different socioeconomic classes. In a country with deep inequalities where there are not many spaces to interact with people from completely different backgrounds, Yo Soy 132 operated as a space for encounters and exchanges. Participants realized that although differentiated, effects and manifestations from a corrupt political system could be felt across income sectors and that persons earlier perceived as enemies could be potential allies.

SOCIAL MEDIA: DEMOCRATIZATION OF INFORMATION AS A MEANS AND AN END

Appreciating the importance of information for democracy and concern about its manipulation by major media outlets was central to the #yosoy132 movement. After a demonstration on May 23, 2011, this was clearly outlined in their list of demands:

> We, the united students of this country, believe that a necessary condition to solve this [political and economic situation] is to empower citizens through information, since it allows us to take better political, economic decisions [. . .] Therefore, Yo Soy 132 takes the right to information and freedom of speech as its main demands.
>
> [. . .] Our movement aims for the democratization of the media, in order to guarantee transparent, plural and impartial information [. . .] which is why we demand real competition in the market of communications [. . .], to make internet access a constitutional right [. . .], to install a code of ethics and an ombudsman in all informative media [. . .] and to broadcast the upcoming presidential debate in all the major television channels with national coverage. (*Animal Político* 2012b)

Informed by a kind of techno-optimism, Castells argues the Internet and social media can build new public spaces where networked communication allows for autonomous and free information exchange and negotiation that will empower citizens, enabling counter-narratives to be developed. Linked to action in urban space, action in digital space can propel social change (Castells 2012). In #yosoy132, digital activism and spontaneous indignation not only quickly filled up the online world, but took over the streets as well, as participants in the movement made clear their demand for democratic use of online spaces, broadcasting, and information services.

Social media was fundamental to the quick emergence of the movement and for its organization. The speed and immediacy of online platforms meant that people could be summoned very quickly to organize the production of videos, demonstrations, assemblies, and other activities. This speed allowed for responses to be both timely and widespread, enabling students to present their own sides of the story and contest the official discourse. Even so, and *contra* Castells's argument, the limitations of online organization also became clear.

As the movement grew and new voices joined in, the needs for effective organization and the complexities of mobilization exceeded the possibilities of relying only on online communication. Although the Internet allows for information to be spread rapidly and through a network, the careful discussion of ideas and consensus-building cannot be done in a diachronic manner, which requires face-to-face meetings. #yosoy132 used social networks to organize, share information among participants and to spread its message, yet it was not limited to these networks.

After several demonstrations, on May 30, 2011, #yosoy132 organized a general assembly involving representatives from fifty-four private and public universities to discuss the political position of the movement. The meeting brought together more than 6,500 people and established clear criteria for participation and membership while positioning the movement as plural, inclusive, pacifist, with no links to any political party and opposed to the imposition of any candidate to the presidency, especially Peña Nieto (Galindo Cáceres and González-Acosta 2013, 99). At that moment, the groups that came together to create #yosoy132 were consolidated as a movement, becoming a political agent with clear demands, position, and procedures. As part of this deliberative process, the #yosoy132 movement agreed to affirm its commitment to nonviolence and the use of nonviolent strategies for the cause.

About nonviolent strategies, the US political scientist Gene Sharp states:

> The oppressed need to learn that they do not need to fight with the oppressors' best weapons. Instead of using violence, they have a greater chance of mobilizing their power capacity by working and acting together using psychological, social, political, and economic weapons- weapons that enable them to become stronger. When they choose these weapons, the oppressed are mobilizing their power in such a way that in the long run the forces of oppression cannot succeed against it. (Sharp and Safieh 1987).

Since the Mexican state was using force through armed security forces backed by their influence over broadcasting and news media, the movement understood that it needed to find sources of power, leverage strategies other than demonstrations to achieve its objectives, and strategies to achieve its objectives. At the same time, the movement wanted to ameliorate the violence of the system and to highlight the links between the government and the big media companies.

The movement used strategies like public speeches, declarations, signed public statements, group petitions, banners, leaflets, pamphlets, vigils, performance arts, marches and protest meetings. According to Sharp's categorization, these actions fall under the rubric of nonviolent *protest and persuasion* (Sharp 1973).

In the July 2011 presidential elections, the National Electoral Institute declared Peña Nieto of the PRI the winner of the election with 38.15 percent of the vote. The runner-up, López Obrador, obtained 31.64 percent of the vote. After the election, the political landscape changed, forcing the #yosoy132 movement to reflect on its ongoing strategy.

What many perceived as the main goal of the movement, that Peña should not win the election, was now irrelevant. It was true, for instance, that many irregularities were documented during the course of the election, especially vote buying, an electoral crime where parties give away money, groceries, and other goods in exchange for a copy of the person's voting identification and a promise to vote for their party. Mexico's mainstream media was typically silent about these crimes and the relevant regulatory bodies were not processing allegations of fraud and vote buying. At that time the #yosoy132 movement was also discussing how to stop Peña from becoming the president: his inauguration was to take place on December 1, 2012. The movement demonstrated at the headquarters of the National Electoral Institute and asked people to send pictures or videos as evidence of electoral irregularities.

Although information and democratization of media around the presidential election were central to the movement, many people focused solely on the figure of Peña Nieto. After the official results of the election became public, the new goal set by the movement was to prevent Enrique Peña Nieto from reaching office on December 1, 2012. Mobilizations continued and legal resources were implemented, yet as the date approached a question lingered in the air: what will happen after this renewed deadline? Once again, it seemed as if we were running against the clock, with no further strategy. Would the movement disappear as spontaneously as it had started?

For some of us, the goal had long before shifted toward political education. We thought it was necessary to imagine and create different ways to engage with politics and not leave decision-making in the hands of a group of people we had elected, or who had reached power through fraud. In line with participative democracy inspired by Zapatistas and other indigenous organizations, our vision to bring about deep transformation was to get more involved in every step of decision-making and implementation of policies.

As the intensity of the conflict rose, the movement did not escalate its confrontation into noncooperation, but continued to engage in a mix of information dissemination and nonviolent protest. This was arguably hardly proportional to the degree of fraud initiated by PRI, which was backed by the silence of the mainstream news broadcasters, and the allegedly "autonomous" electoral agencies. Leaflets describing Gene Sharp's "198 methods of non-violent action" (Sharp 1973) were circulated among the students. This information had no context and the organizing groups did not deeply reflect on the leaflets use or on the implications of doing this. This inability to process information into knowledge hindered the movement from employing tactics of nonviolent dissent into a more appropriate or effective kind of politics.

While most student participants in the movement advocated for a strategy without violence (i.e., without exerting physical force over others or damage private property), some people in the movement did smash windows and graffitied on walls. The movement officially did not condone these actions, yet the openness to participate in demonstrations did not allow for control over everyone's actions. In those moments, it was difficult to determine when actions that deflected from nonviolence were indeed executed by demonstrators or by undercover government agents (Plascencia 2012).

Regardless of provocations and isolated cases, the movement remained largely nonviolent, and we thought this would protect us from repression. When we realized that the force exerted by the government against demonstrators was not proportional to our actions, it became clear to us how repressive the government's reactions were. For many people who were not previously involved in social justice movements, it became obvious that government repression in Mexico was a reality and the criminalization of social protest through distorted information on the media was unveiled.

The Mexican state exercised no equivalent restraint. Several members of the #yosoy132 movement were beaten up by police, while others were subjected to threats, arbitrary detention, and even disappearance. With the help of human rights organizations, we learned the need to document human rights violations and violence from government agents. Repression became an unavoidable reality that society was no longer able to avoid or justify.

DEMOCRACY THROUGH DEMOCRATIC MEANS

#yosoy132 is grounded in a long tradition of student movements that can be traced back to 1968 and the "Massacre of Tlatelolco," when the federal PRI government killed at least 400 young protesters in the Plaza de las Tres Culturas in Mexico City (Heraldo de México 2019). The activities organized in UNAM were quickly joined by people who had participated in the 1999 student strike and still had some connection to the university. In a way, this participation shaped both the demands and the movement's program which absorbed this history into the movement. At the same time, UNAM students were also able to learn from their own practices, including their mistakes and their achievements. For instance, it became clear that while it was important to decentralize power and take decisions collectively, face-to-face meetings still played a crucial role.

Inspired by the 1999 student strike, direct democracy was embraced as a fundamental principle and the assembly system was adopted by the movement (Oprinari 2016, 206–208). Each school or college became an organizational cell. There were no leaders who made decisions vertically on behalf of the whole movement or even on behalf of school assemblies. The general assembly was the main site for decision-making, where representatives of school assemblies presented and discussed the resolutions agreed upon in local assemblies, to later return the results of the general assembly for each school to ratify. These representatives were called *spokespersons*, a role that could be revoked and that needed to be constantly rotated among different participants of each school.

This process was long and many wanted to speed up the deliberative process to accelerate action. The decision-making process took place through long assemblies that sometimes ran for more than twelve hours and had to be rescheduled for the following day. In addition to the time invested in assemblies and demonstrations were the internal meetings of committees and their work, such as screening documentaries publicly, organizing artistic performances, informing people in public spaces about what was happening, using megaphones.

This was a constant source of debate between students in public schools, who participated in the 1999 strike, and students from private schools, who had been taught at school about the representative conception of democracy. The material realities became inescapable, and those who had family or employment responsibilities diminished their rate of participation. Regardless of this, the deliberative process adopted ensured that there were no leaders or factions to be co-opted, that the movement was genuinely following the course of what the majority decided and that every voice had an opportunity to be heard.

Although the movement started with students, we quickly recognized the need to involve other groups, not only to expand the level of public support but to know more about their needs and to invite them to organize. We set up activities like information brigades, for which we printed material and talked with people in the streets to learn about their opinions. We also let people know what we wanted to achieve. We projected presidential debates in public squares and facilitated discussion groups as a way of spreading information out to people who might not have had access to social media. Neighborhoods and communities formed their own assemblies and were then granted a vote in the General Inter-University Assembly.

Apart from assemblies, special committees were formed. For instance, the Arts and Cultures Committees or the Legal and Human Rights Committee, which had the important role of documenting, exposing and pressing charges in respect of crimes committed against demonstrators and monitoring their security. There was a space for every person to apply the knowledge acquired from their discipline.

MEDIA AND SOCIETY RESPONSES

Being accustomed to union movements, which typically have a clear leader, the Mexican state and mainstream media were disturbed and surprised to find that there was no leader of #yosoy132 to negotiate with and get information from. It is true that some active and highly visible members of the movement were represented as leaders, though in reality they were not the ones who made decisions: the assemblies did, because the general assembly was the supreme organ.

One example of this was Antonio Attolini, a political science student who infamously seized the opportunity to land a job as an "expert" on a television show produced by Televisa. While many considered Attolini's recruitment a betrayal on his part of the movement, it also highlighted Televisa's need to quickly recoup some of the credibility it had lost. By recruiting one of the better-known "faces" of the #yosoy132 movement, it portrayed an image to its audience of their inclusivity of opinions even as it tried to discredit the movement. In this respect, it was too late.

#yosoy132 received tremendous support from many people in Mexico and abroad. Part of the organizing activities of the movement included talking with people in the streets. Musicians, filmmakers, and the artistic community in general spoke positively about the movement through their platforms. Support groups were formed by Mexicans residing in various cities abroad, especially in the United Kingdom, the United States, Spain, and Canada (Informador Mx 2012).

Following the demands of the movement, Televisa agreed to broadcast the second presidential debate organized by the Federal Electoral Institute. Broadcasted online, #yosoy132 organized a presidential debate that took place on June 19, making the headline of every newspaper in the country the following day (Morales 2014, 156–165). The movement was relevant enough to convince all candidates but the PRI candidate Peña Nieto to participate.

VIOLENT STATE RESPONSE TO THE #YOSOY132 MOVEMENT

In Mexico, the right to protest is guaranteed by international human rights laws, beginning with the Universal Declaration of Human Rights (1948), and ratified by the Mexican State in the Mexican Constitution. The demonstrations organized by #yosoy132 were nonviolent. Yet, the human rights commission set up to investigate the movement reported some seventy well-documented cases of assaults and violence against members. It also claimed that many more cases had occurred but were not reported because of fear of repercussions. Among other things, students were arbitrarily detained, beaten, harassed, threatened, and robbed. Some assaults were carried out by police and some by members of Partido Revolucionario Institutional in states where that party was in government (Castro Bribiesca 2012).

According to Max Weber "the state is a relation of men dominating men, a relation supported by means of legitimate (i.e. considered to be legitimate) violence. If the state is to exist, the dominated must obey the authority claimed by the powers that be" (Weber 1958, 78). Around the sources of this foundation of legitimacy, he claims that one of them is legality: "there is domination by virtue of 'legality,' by virtue of the belief in the validity of legal statute and functional 'competence' based on rationally created rules" (Weber 1958, 79).

If we were to accept Weber's account of legitimacy and legality, how could we make sense of the use of violence by the Mexican state in this context? If the demonstrators were not using physical force and were not posing a threat to the governance of the country, the lives of others, and there was no threat to public assets, was the use of force from the government justified? If the government acts extra-legally by not respecting the right to demonstrate, what then, is the source of its legitimacy?

The repression by the government and its condoning of violence enacted by its own personnel or that of other actors against members of the #yosoy132 movement highlighted the disproportionate use of violence by the Mexican government. Middle- and upper-middle-class families, who had not traditionally been involved with social action and social justice movements, were confronted by a situation where questions about the legitimacy of the state could not be avoided.

HOPE AND DISILLUSION FROM THE MOBILIZATIONS

#yosoy132 inspired many to believe in the possibility of democratic change. It was referred to as the "Mexican Spring," an unexpected nonviolent revolution brought about by students that would once and for all transform the political system. After the declaration of Peña Nieto's victory and violent police repression during Inauguration Day, this hope took a beating, as if it had been all for nothing. If the expectation was that Peña Nieto would not become president and yet he had done so, what did the period of struggle mean?

Although the movement was relevant enough to raise questions about the alleged "neutrality" and impartiality of the mass media and also persuaded the presidential candidates to engage in an independently organized and independently broadcast electoral debate, this did not prevent the PRI from regaining power. It did not stop the media from spreading "fake news." By 2013, the political and moral credibility of the #yosoy132 movement was depleted and internal discord prevailed, resulting in a split of the movement.

According to Álvarez Brunel, an activist in the movement, there were other strategies to demobilize protesters. From within the movement, external agents infiltrated and tried to generate internal division. Hostile agents were embedded into assemblies and demonstrations to cause chaos and promote the idea that the movement faced an "invincible enemy." These agents spread the idea that the #yosoy132 movement was disorganized and erratic, and worse that it was linked to opposition parties (Álvarez Brunel 2016). These actions were designed to spread disillusionment within the movement and to diminish its support base.

In terms of the result of the elections, what #yosoy132 did is too complex to be evaluated simply as "success" or "failure." For many, it was a space of awakening and learning, for networking and experimentation. A lot of learning on the part of students happened outside the classroom, with many theories being questioned and put into practice. After the General Assembly dissolved in early 2013, many participants continued to reflect on what happened and imagine other ways of organizing to continue intervening in the political realm. The legacy of the movement can be found in the visible effects it had at the time, but also in the initiatives that came directly from it.

LESSONS AND LEGACY

For Olivier Téllez and Tamargo (2015), the main achievement of the #yosoy132 movement was that it outlined a new model of organization that went beyond the traditional organizational forms adopted by political parties. This seems right but the achievement also extends to its effect on the work of its members outside of the movement.

Alonso (2013) argues that the legacy of the movement lies in creative innovations for democracy. These include, for example, decentralizing the movement, the techniques used to achieve consensus and dealing with dissent, its exercise of autonomy by determining its own processes, its search for horizontality without designated leaders and its use of alternating spokespersons. According to Alonso, part of its success came from its constant dialogue with other popular organizations that enabled the transfer of the experience of people who had been organizing and building a grass-roots democratic base for years. The real significance of the movement lies in the ways it drew from the practical wisdom of indigenous groups whose members collectively explored alternatives to representative democracy.

The movement was smart and humble enough to recognize the experience and wisdom of other movements like the Spanish *Indignados*, and skillful enough to communicate their message to people who had not had this experience. Similarly, the movement was empathetic and sensible enough to read the importance of observing the violence that was being directed at other movements and to understand that what other movements were combating was as important as their own struggles. As Jenny Pearce, a British expert on violence in Latin America states:

> Recognising the vulnerable body is not an abstract process. Hence, acknowledging the way social action increasingly puts this onto the public agenda enables us to imagine a politics whose tasks are not best resolved by violence. Such action includes, for instance, mobilisation by sections of society across more and more cultures against abuse in the intimate sphere of social life and naming it as violence. Politics itself can become a field where the conditions to live without violence can be struggled over. (2017, 2)

Another important lesson the movement learned was the need to think "outside the box," to manage the ethical and political energy of participants and transcend conventional models of political participation. I spent a great deal of the next months after May 2012 in every demonstration and assembly. I went to other towns to participate in activist camps. I pushed myself to the limit and felt as if I was indispensable to the campaign, as if not being at any given activity implied a lack of commitment on my part. I abandoned other projects and left areas of my life unattended (particularly my studies) to devote energy and time to the movement. I do not regret my choices, as I understand how crucial they were for my political education and yet I would have liked to find ways of linking the lectures that were part of my formal education with my practice within the movement. I would have appreciated, for instance, if teachers had adapted the lectures to actually talk about what was going on in our organization and not keep the lessons abstract and theoretical.

By October 2012, I was suffering from serious burnout and frustration. Physically and emotionally, I could not continue to be completely involved anymore. Although my participation continued, it was at a considerably lower intensity. Many other students similarly suffered burnouts. Within Yo Soy 132, people in assemblies would distribute tasks and committees would be formed. However, a crucial lesson we learned from this was to rethink the possibilities for fighting the campaign. Where can each of us serve the cause best and most strategically? Evidently, the answer is different for every person and this diversity, when organized, is a great source of strength.

Former members of the movement organized independent initiatives. Political hubs were developed by former members of the movement. An example of this is Wikipolítica, the platform of Pedro Kumamoto, who, at 27 years old, became the first independent candidate to be elected for the Congress of Jalisco, his home state. If the mainstream media was monopolized by the government, certain groups within the movement understood the answer was not to ask the media itself to become more democratic, but to create genuine alternative information platforms. Others decided to create independent media, like Nación 321, a digital news and entertainment platform.

Within the movement, we had a direct experience of how activists can replicate violence, thus recognizing the need for continuous internal-critique. Seeing racism, classism, misogyny, and homophobia reproduced in some of the activities enacted within the movement we were so invested in felt both disappointing and instructive. Offensive chants like *Peña Puto* (Peña, faggot) and other expressions of homophobia, helped us realize the need for revision and deconstruction of culturally learned and reproduced beliefs and attitudes. From these understanding, collectives within the movement became vocal, particularly feminist groups.

Through #yosoy132, we met, gathered, and became empowered. Some people, now in the grip of apathy, ask themselves where the energy that took them to streets in 2012 is now. The movement did not die but changed shape. It did not disappear but transformed many of its participants and Mexican society. Although #yosoy132 as a cohesive group is no longer organizing actions, its effects can be observed in the way a younger generation is participating in politics and the sensibility that was developed around social action.

THE EFFECTS OF #YOSOY132 ON NATIONAL POLITICS

The movement's constant work was to contest state-sponsored political and structural violence in a nonviolent way. In doing this, it mobilized a sector of society that had not been traditionally involved in social movements, contested mainstream narratives that described Mexican media as impartial and objective, and provoked the state into using violence, even against the middle class.

After #yosoy132, the violence and repression of student activists were firmly placed at the center of the discussion, along with the importance of education and of establishing solidarity with other movements. According to Moissen, the best proof of youth politicization opened up by #yosoy132 was solidarity with the strike of Coordinadora Nacional de Trabajadores de la Educación, the teachers' union fighting changes to educational laws which infringed their labor rights (Moissen 2014, 241–242). In the same way, #yosoy132 and the narratives around it promoted and mobilized popular anger in 2014 following the Ayotzinapa Massacre, when forty-three rural students were "disappeared." Much of the organization of these demonstrations relied on #yosoy132 and people's awareness of the power of organizing in both the online world and in public spaces.

The image of Peña Nieto and of Televisa, severely damaged by the movement, continued to decay during Peña Nieto's presidential term. Aided by the proliferation of online informative and entertainment alternatives, the movement played a crucial role in Televisa's loss of popularity. The movement managed to highlight the issue of the information duopoly in Mexico. A law on telecommunication was discussed and passed during Nieto's term, regarded by many as a simulation that mostly benefited telecommunications tycoon Carlos Slim.

Following Ayotzinapa, Peña Nieto's popularity sagged. The continued perception of him being incompetent, ignorant, and corrupt owed a lot to the movement. In the presidential election, taking place in 2018, the PRI lost to the 2006 and 2012 runner-up, Andrés Manuel López Obrador, whose popularity owes to some extent to the work of #yosoy132 though documenting this will have to be subject of another study.

CONCLUSION

#yosoy132 encouraged the political education of a generation. It began as a spontaneous expression of indignation and developed into a movement encompassing more than 100 universities throughout the country enjoying wide national and international support. It managed to learn from popular movements that had been exploring alternative political options for decades and was able to translate them into middle-class and urban practices as a part of its legacy.

In the context of the 2012 presidential election, the #yosoy132 movement denounced the support that major broadcasters had given to the PRI, a party that had amassed great power during the seventy years it had held the presidential post. Persons who were traditionally not involved in social justice movements realized their rights were being violated and rose up, later becoming victims themselves of censorship and repression, which encouraged empathy to develop around other causes and demonstrating groups.

Thanks to social media, the #yosoy132 movement grew quickly and its message was spread, contesting official narratives. While the power of online organization was crucial to the emergence of the movement, action in public spaces was, in turn, fundamental. Demonstrations, organizational spaces, and dialogue with diverse agents were central to the activities of #yosoy132. While demanding democracy, the movement learned from other organizational experiences the importance of being coherent and adopting democratic methods. Although assemblies required a considerable time investment, they provided valuable lessons about the benefits and level of commitment required for direct democracy.

The movement adopted a nonviolent approach to social action. The response of the government to peaceful demonstrations was not proportional in terms of strength and the violence used, repressing students and violating their right to demonstrate. There were clear intentions to tarnish its reputation and demobilize participants through exterminating hope and installing fear through repression.

Open to learning and experimenting, #yosoy132 was nourished by the experience of other activists and by its involvement with other social justice movements. #yosoy132 eventually dissolved into different projects, and its legacy is evident in other political proposals like political hubs and independent candidacies, alternative media and the potential of its networks, which are still very much alive.

Far from idealizing the movement, the best way of learning about it is by being critical and reflecting on its setbacks. Learning to organize takes time and especially participatory and direct democracy takes patience and trust in the process, which many in the movement lacked. The legacy of Yo Soy 132 should not only be assessed in terms of accomplishment of its goals. The effects it had in Mexico, the lessons learned by participants, the networks created and projects that stemmed from it are equally relevant and will doubtlessly be the subject of study in the future.

REFERENCES

Alonso, Jorge. 2013. 'Cómo escapar de la cárcel de lo electoral: el movimiento #yosoy132.' *Desacatos* 42: 17–40. https://doi.org/10.29340/42.67.

Álvarez Brunel, Emmanuel. 2016. '#YoSoy132: proceso de construcción de la esperanza.' In *¿Cómo construir la paz en el México actual?*, edited by Pietro Ameglio and Tania Ramírez, 419–432. Mexico City: Plaza y Valdéz/Universidad del Claustro de Sor Juana.

Animal Político. 2012a. 'Encuesta de Reforma pone a López Obrador a 4 puntos de Peña Nieto.' 31 May 2012. https://www.animalpolitico.com/2012/05/encuesta-de-reforma-pone-a-lopez-obrador-a-4-puntos-de-pena-nieto/.

Animal Político. 2012b. 'Yo Soy 132. Declaratoria y pliego petitorio.' 23 May 2012. https://www.animalpolitico.com/2012/05/declaratoria-y-pliego-petitorio-de-yo-soy-132/.

Castells, Manuel. 2012. *Networks of Outrage and Hope—Social Movements in the Internet Age*. Chichester: Wiley.

Castro Bribiesca, Sergio Adrián. 2012. '#YoSoy132, la geografía de la represión.' *Desinformémonos*, 30 September 2012. https://desinformemonos.org/represion-132/.

El País. 2006. 'Más de un millón de personas apoyan a López Obrador en la Plaza del Zócalo en México.' 31 July 2006. https://elpais.com/internacional/2006/07/31/actualidad/1154296802_850215.html.

Galindo Cáceres, Jesús, and José Ignacio González-Acosta. 2013. *#YoSoy132. La primera erupción visible*. Mexico City: Global Talent University Press. http://editorialrazonypalabra.org/pdf/palabra-otros/Galindo_YoSoy132.pdf.

Heraldo de México. 2019. 'Cronología: Así fue la matanza del 2 de octubre de 1968 en Tlatelolco.' 2 October 2019. https://heraldodemexico.com.mx/pais/cronologia-asi-fue-la-matanza-2-octubre-1968-tlatelolco-masacre-plaza-de-las-tres-culturas-cronica/.

Informador Mx. '#YoSoy132 cuenta con 52 asambleas internacionales.' 1 August 2012. https://www.informador.mx/Mexico/YoSoy132-cuenta-con-52-asambleas-internacionales-20120801-0102.html.

Moissen, Sergio. 2016. 'Del #YoSoy132 al apoyo a la lucha magisterial.' In *#juventudenlascalles. 68.99.YoSoy132*, edited by Sergio Moissen, 225–244. Mexico City: Armas de la Crítica. https://massimomodonesi.files.wordpress.com/2014/08/296112606-sergio-moissen-et-al-juventud-en-las-calles-68-99-yosoy132-pdf.pdf.

Morales Sierra, Federico. 2014. 'El movimiento estudiantil #YoSoy132. Antología hemerográfica.' MA Thesis, Universidad Iberoamericana Ciudad de México. http://www.bib.uia.mx/tesis/pdf/015937/015937.pdf.

Olivier Téllez, Guadalupe, and Sergio Tamayo. 2015. 'Tensiones políticas en el proceso de movilización-desmovilización: El movimiento #YoSoy132.' *Iztapalapa, Revista de ciencias sociales y humanidades* 79: 131–170. https://www.redalyc.org/articulo.oa?id=39348248009.

Oprinari, Pablo. 2016. 'Apuntes sobre la huelga de fin de siglo.' In *#juventudenlascalles. 68.99.YoSoy132*, edited by Sergio Moissen, 185–210. Mexico City: Armas de la Crítica. https://massimomodonesi.files.wordpress.com/2014/08/296112606-sergio-moissen-et-al-juventud-en-las-calles-68-99-yosoy132-pdf.pdf.

Ortega Olivares, Mario. 2010. 'Movimiento estudiantil, clase y subjetividad.' *Veredas. Revista del Pensamiento Sociológico* 11(21): 129–147.

Pearce, Jenny. 2017. 'The Demonic Genius of Politics? Social Action and Decoupling of Politics from Violence.' *International Journal of Conflict and Violence* 11: 1–11. https://doi.org/10.4119/UNIBI/ijcv.624.

Plascencia, Ángel. 2012. '¿Se detuvo a los provocadores?' *Reporte Índigo*, 10 December 2012. https://www.reporteindigo.com/reporte/se-detuvo-los-provocadores/.

Rojas, Ana Gabriela. 2018. 'Caso Atenco: CorteIDH sentencia a México por violencia sexual, violación y tortura a 11 mujeres.' *BBC News*, 21 December 2018. https://www.bbc.com/mundo/noticias-america-latina-46656044.

Sharp, Gene. 1973. *The Politics of Nonviolent Action*. Boston: Porter Sargent.

Sharp, Gene, and Afif Safieh. 1987. 'Gene Sharp: Nonviolent Struggle'. *Journal of Palestine Studies* 17(1): 37–55. https://jps.ucpress.edu/content/17/1/37.

Vapormipatria. 2012. 'Cómo nace Yo soy 132 Video original de yo soy 131.' 1 November 2012. Video, 10:59. https://www.youtube.com/watch?v=hca6lzoE2z8.

Weber, Max. 1958. 'Politics as a Vocation'. In *From Max Weber: Essays in Sociology*, edited and translated by Hans Heinrich Gerth and Charles Wright Mills, 77–128. New York: Oxford University Press.

Index

About the Contributors

Enzo Bello
Enzo Bello is a full professor at the Law School of the Universidade Federal Fluminense (UFF), Brazil. He holds a Ph.D. in law from the Universidade do Estado do Rio de Janeiro (UERJ), Brazil and is the chief editor of the *Revista Culturas Jurídicas / Legal Cultures Journal.*

Judith Bessant
Judith Bessant is a Member of the Order of Australia, a professor at RMIT University, and an adjunct professor at the School of Justice, QUT, Australia. She publishes in the areas of history, sociology, politics, youth studies, and media studies.

Gustavo Capela
Gustavo Capela is a Ph.D. student in the Department of Anthropology at the University of California, Berkeley, USA. He holds a master's degree in law from Universidade de Brasilia (UnB), Brazil.

Sofia Donoso
Sofia Donoso is an assistant professor at the Department of Sociology of the Universidad de Chile. She holds a Ph.D. in Development Studies from the University of Oxford, UK. She is the coeditor of *Social Movements in Chile: Organization, Trajectories, and Political Consequences* (Palgrave MacMillan, 2017).

Joseph Egwurube
Joseph Egwurube was a senior lecturer in public administration for several years at Ahmadu Bello University, Zaria, in Nigeria. He teaches today at La Rochelle University in France.

Carlos de Jesús Gómez-Abarca
Carlos de Jesús Gómez-Abarca holds a Ph.D. in social and humanistic sciences from the Universidad de Ciencias y Artes de Chiapas. He is the chief investigator of the Observatorio de las Democracias: Sur de México y Centroamérica—Centro de Estudios Superiores de México y Centroamérica (Chiapas, México).

Meena Kandiah
Meena Kandiah holds postgraduate degrees in sociology, criminology, and education from the UK. Her research interests revolve around Tamil diaspora politics.

Rene José Keller
Rene Keller holds a Ph.D. in law from the Universidade do Estado do Rio de Janeiro (UERJ), Brazil, as well as a Ph.D. in social work from the Pontifícia Universidade Católica do Rio Grande de Sul (PUCRS), Brazil.

Analicia Mejia Mesinas
Analicia Mejia Mesinas holds a Ph.D. in criminology, law and society, from the University of California, Irvine, USA. She is an assistant professor in the Department of Criminal Justice at Azusa Pacific University. Her research if focused on youth activism, police in schools, and the criminalization of youth.

Sarah Pickard
Sarah Pickard is a senior lecturer and researcher (MCF HDR) at Université Sorbonne Nouvelle—Paris 3. Her research is on young people's political participation, especially emerging forms of engagement, such as Do-It-Ourselves (DIO) politics and she authored *Politics, Protest and Young People* (Palgrave Macmillan, 2019).

Pablo Santibáñez-Rodríguez
Pablo Santibáñez-Rodríguez is a doctoral student in the Department of Education, Practice and Society at the Institute of Education, University College London, UK. His work as a researcher and teacher covers the area of youth studies and their implications for education, policy, and politics.

Nicolás Somma

Nicolás Somma is an associate professor at the Institute of Sociology of the Pontificia Universidad Católica de Chile and is a research fellow, Centre for Social Conflict and Cohesion Studies (COES).

Nisha Thapliyal

Nisha Thapliyal is a senior lecturer in comparative and international education at the University of Newcastle, Australia. Her research areas include social movements for public education and rights-based education policy in India, Brazil, and the United States.

Lorna Zamora Robles

Lorna Zamora Robles is a Human Rights and Peace educator and community organizer. She holds a degree in intercultural development and conflict transformation. Her work and research revolve around issues of social justice, identity, globalization, peace, and embodiment.

www.ingramcontent.com/pod-product-compliance
Lightning Source LLC
Chambersburg PA
CBHW021820270326
41932CB00007B/265
* 9 7 9 8 8 8 1 8 0 1 0 2 1 *